STRANGE TALES OF THE DARK AND BLOODY GROUND

STRANGE TALES OF THE DARK AND BLOODY GROUND

Authentic Accounts of Restless Spirits, Haunted Honky-Tonks, and Eerie Events in Tennessee

Christopher Kiernan Coleman

RUTLEDGE HILL PRESS®
Nashville, Tennessee

Copyright © 1998 by Christopher Kiernan Coleman

Published in Nashville, Tennessee, by Rutledge Hill Press®, 211 Seventh Avenue North, Nashville, Tennessee 37219.
Distributed in Canada by H. B. Fenn & Company, Ltd., 34 Nixon Road, Bolton, Ontario L7E 1W2.
Distributed in Australia by The Five Mile Press Pty., Ltd., 22 Summit Road, Noble Park, Victoria 3174.
Distributed in New Zealand by Tandem Press, 2 Rugby Road, Birkenhead, Auckland 10.
Distributed in the United Kingdom by Verulam Publishing, Ltd., 152a Park Street Lane, Park Street, Saint Albans, Hertfordshire AL2 2AU.

Typography by E. T. Lowe, Nashville, Tennessee

Library of Congress Cataloging-in-Publication Data

Strange tales of the dark and bloody ground : authentic accounts of restless spirits, haunted honky-tonks, and eerie events in Tennessee /
    [compiled by] Christopher Kiernan Coleman.
        p.   cm.
    ISBN 1-55853-661-2 (pbk.)
    1. Ghosts-Tennessee.   I. Coleman, Christopher Kiernan, 1949–   .
BF1472.U6S77   1998
133.1'29768—dc21   98-34829
                                                                          CIP

Printed in the United States of America

1 2 3 4 5 6 7 8 9 — 02 01 00 99 98

To my wonderful wife, Veronica, the light of my life;
and to my son Chris Jr.,
who inspired me to write this book.

ACKNOWLEDGMENTS

I WISH TO THANK ALL THE INFORMANTS who told me of their experiences with the Other Realm; the staff of the Nashville Public Library—especially those in the Area Resource Center, the Nashville Room, and the Reference Department; and the staff of the Tennessee State Library & Archives. Without all their help, this book would not have been possible.

CONTENTS

INTRODUCTION

WELCOME TO TRANSYLVANIA: THE DARK AND BLOODY GROUND

PERHAPS IT IS THE ABUNDANCE OF DECAY-
ing mansions in the South that all seem to keep some
deep and sinister secret, or perhaps it is the South's tragic
history—its heritage of war and defeat. Or, it may just be
the average southerner's love of a good story that accounts for the fact that the South is so steeped in tales of
the supernatural and the strange.

The fact is, there is hardly a community throughout
the southland that does not have its haunted house or resident hobgoblin. Some parts of the South, however, seem
particularly favored by fate in this regard. The Mid-South
is one such region. From the verdant hills and vales of the
Smokies to the broad, meandering meadows of the Cumberland and Tennessee Valleys to the rich red-clay cotton
fields of West Tennessee and the Mississippi Valley, the
beauty of the land belies a strange and unearthly heritage.

Although Tennessee and the Mid-South have long
been favored by providence with an abundance of good
things, there is a darker side to this land—a deadly bless-
ing, if you will. Beyond the beauty and the bounty of the
land and the friendly ways of its people, there lies another realm that lurks just beyond the twilight.

This land, this other realm, is the abode of restless

spirits, uncanny gifts from the sky, whirlwinds of fire, bewitched farmers, and haunted honky-tonks. If such a curious—or cursed—domain brings to mind images of the haunted land of ancient Transylvania rather than the American South, one would not be so far from the truth. For, by strange coincidence, at one time a large portion of the Mid-South was in fact called Transylvania.

When the first white settlers came over the mountains to these new and strange western woodlands, they regarded it as a kind of "wilderado"—a wilderness El Dorado—a fabled realm filled with the promise of adventure and wealth. While to these early pioneers the region held little dread or doom, for their Native American neighbors it was a far different story.

To the Indians—who had already lived here for eons uncounted—this land was a place of awe and mystery. It was a strange and sacred realm where the supernatural was natural and where anything might happen.

Aside from a small part of southeastern Tennessee and neighboring areas of Georgia and North Carolina where the Cherokee dwelt, and the regions of northern Mississippi and southwestern Tennessee where the Chickasaws lived, most of this vast domain lay vacant. Why did the Indians choose not to dwell here?

Once upon a time they did. Long before the white man came, a great and mighty civilization flourished in the Mid-South, raising pyramids and massive burial mounds, and building large earthen fortresses and towns the equal of medieval Europe's. Yet all this was gone by the time the white man arrived. What unknown dread could have fallen upon the land to cause the Ancient Ones to abandon their homes?

All that is known for certain is that, for as long as the tribes could remember, a strict taboo forbade anyone from settling in the region, on pain of dire punishment. Only the white man was fool enough to break this taboo.

But a taboo of another sort faced the first white settlers: King George had forbidden them to settle on the other side of the mountains. Ignoring his command, however, they bought a large tract of wilderness from the Indians. In 1775, white men and red sat down to parley at Sycamore Shoals, now a part of East Tennessee. In exchange for a bounty of trade goods, Cherokee leaders sold an enormous tract of wilderness, most of what is now the Mid-South. The white land speculators who bought it called it Transylvania, which literally means "across the woods."

Not all the Indians agreed to the sale, however. During the several days of parleying, each chief in turn got up to speak. For the most part, they were agreeable to giving the whites the vacant land. If they could not live on it, why not sell it to the land-hungry whites?

But one proud chief disagreed. Dragging Canoe was his name, and he was the nephew of the great Attakullakulla, the legendary leader of the Cherokees. Dragging Canoe did not share his uncle's love of peace or his willingness to compromise with the whites; he had come not to condone the proceedings but to condemn them. Speaking in measured but stern tones, his tongue cut sharper than a tomahawk's edge—and spared no one.

Condemning the whites for their all-consuming greed, and his own people for their folly, he boldly reminded the chiefs that they were trading away sacred land, land that ought not be defiled by the white man's ax and plow.

"This is the Dark and Bloody Ground!" he finally declared. He paused for effect, then repeated his words as his hawk-like gaze penetrated each of the sitting chiefs in turn. Then Dragging Canoe fell silent; he turned his back on the proceedings and left.

Dragging Canoe's words were unsettling—were they meant as prophecy, curse, or threat? No one is quite sure. The whites were bewildered, but the Indians refused to explain what the proud chief had meant. What is known is that a short time after he uttered those words of doom, they began to come true.

A year later, Attakullakulla was dead, and the very leaders who had sat down in peace were at war with one another. Red man fought white, as the Indians sided with the British during the Revolution. But the bloodshed did not end when America gained its independence; for some twenty years after that, the southern tribes fought the whites. And for their efforts, their villages were burned and their women and children went hungry. For the whites, the scalping knife and tomahawk were ever-present threats. Raid followed counter-raid for a generation as the two sides slaughtered one another with abandon. The new land of Transylvania had indeed become the Dark and Bloody Ground.

In the end, the Indians who had traded away the taboo lands of their ancestors would be driven from their homeland. But the white victors would not enjoy the fruits of their conquest for long as civil war fell upon the land, and the Dark and Bloody Ground earned its name all over again.

But beyond all these man-made misfortunes—and natural disasters—the land has seen more than its fair share of supernatural misfortune. From the earliest times, it seems, the mysterious and inexplicable have haunted the Mid-South—more so than most people have realized.

Are all of these strange incidents the result of Dragging Canoe's curse? Is some other malevolent force at work instead? Or is it all simply accident piled upon coincidence, as government officials and many academics would have us believe?

In the following pages, you will encounter documented cases of strange and inexplicable phenomena—chance encounters with the Dark and Bloody Ground. The facts are presented as truthfully and accurately as possible.

All of the tales are authentic. If some incidents seem incredible, that is because they are—but they are no less true for all of that. What interpretation one chooses to give them, however, is another matter. That we leave up to you.

So read on, but proceed with caution, dear reader. You have already entered the realm of the Dark and Bloody Ground—the South's very own Transylvania!

APPALACHIAN APPARITIONS: STRANGE TALES OF THE MOUNTAINS

1

Tom Brown's Ghoul Days: A Spectral Tour of Rugby, Tennessee

RUGBY. THE VERY NAME EVOKES IMAGES of the playing fields of Eton and all things English. On first arriving in Rugby, Tennessee, the town does not disappoint. One has the uncanny feeling of having been suddenly transported as if by magic to a quaint British village of another era.

Nestled in a small scenic valley high on the Cumberland Plateau, Rugby's charming streets and cozy cottages exude an aura of Victorian England. This pleasant, placid veneer makes it hard to believe that the very same community has often been described as "one of the most haunted towns in America."

Without a doubt, the spirit and charm of the age of Victoria lies heavy on this picturesque hamlet. Indeed, a number of Victorian Englishmen liked it so much, their spirits never left. Even without its resident phantoms, however, the story of Rugby would still be a most unusual one.

Rugby was founded in the 1880s by the acclaimed English novelist Thomas Hughes, author of the morbidly sentimental novel *Tom Brown's School Days*. It was Hughes's cherished dream to establish a utopian community here. He envisioned Rugby as a place where the idle younger sons of British nobility could come to experience the virtues of honest labor in an atmosphere of high morality and culture.

In the late nineteenth century, England's inheritance laws apparently still favored the eldest son. The senior male child inherited all of the land, wealth, and titles, leaving nothing of the father's estate for the younger siblings. Not only were younger sons reduced to living off their elder brother's charity, they also were even prohibited by custom from engaging in any gainful employment considered beneath the dignity and status of a "gentleman."

Outside of the clergy or the army—neither of which paid very well—younger male heirs had no useful role in Victorian society. More often than not, they ended up idle and dissolute, continually leeching off friends and family to maintain their lifestyle.

Thomas Hughes and other like-minded philanthropists conceived the idea of creating a haven for these idle young men in America, where such rigid social strictures did not apply. Hughes hoped these young scions might thereby avoid the sloth and moral degeneracy he found so common among the London gentry of his day.

At first, Thomas Hughes's "Distant Eden" seemed as though it would blossom into a thriving community. A suitable location was secured in the scenic wilderness of Tennessee's Cumberland Plateau, donations were secured, and young Englishmen began arriving almost daily to join the utopian community.

In the end, however, Hughes's vision came to naught. The location, while beautiful, was too remote to be viable commercially. It also transpired that the majority of young gentry in England preferred their idle ways to the rigors of hard labor in the New World. Moreover, many who did come to Rugby found its stern moral code—and prohibition of alcohol—overly constricting.

One other problem the well-meaning sponsors of Rugby had not foreseen was the lack of appropriate female companions for the young men. Single Englishwomen from good families had little inclination to relocate, and the local girls were not regarded as suitable by the blue-blooded benefactors of the colony. In fact, about the only British women who came to reside in Rugby were those who were already married.

This peculiar—and volatile—state of affairs may in fact have been the underlying cause of an incident that led to the town's first documented haunting.

The Tabard Inn was erected in 1882 by the colony in order to accommodate visitors and new arrivals. It was a pleasant enough hostelry, with a large mansard roof and wide verandahs on both the first and second stories. The third story sat atop the structure like a peaked crown, its ornate grillwork and small arched windows sparkling like jewels in the sun. Inside, the main staircase was reputed to contain a baluster from its namesake—the Tabard Inn of Chaucer's day. The hotel was destroyed by fire within a few days of Halloween 1884—under mysterious circumstances.

But the Tabard Inn arose phoenix-like from the ashes. Rebuilt on an even grander scale, the new hotel included a spacious lounge where the "sacred log" from the ancient Tabard Inn's balustrade was displayed in a glass case over the mantle, the venerable relic having been rescued from the flames of the original Rugby inn.

The first manager of the rebuilt inn had been a British sea captain, an amiable old salt of whom everyone was fond. After a time, however, he hoisted anchor and made sail for another port of call. The captain was replaced my a Mr. Davis, late of Buffalo, New York.

In the southwest corner of the second floor of the new inn was Room 13. Although a pleasant room, it was shunned by guests as unlucky. Room 13 often remained empty even when the rest of the inn was full. Mr. Davis, therefore, moved himself and his beautiful young wife into the room, using it as their own abode.

On New Year's Eve 1897, Davis and his wife held a grand ball in the hotel. The cream of society from Rugby and the surrounding region were all invited to attend. The large lobby served as ballroom, and a brass band from nearby Harriman provided the music. The dancing commenced at eight and continued till the stroke of midnight, when all in attendance held hands and sang "Auld Lang Syne." The guests warmly wished one another a Happy New Year.

It has been suggested that perhaps one of the young and handsome Englishmen may have become a trifle too ardent in wishing the young Mrs. Davis joy for the coming year—and that she may have been only too happy to return the favor.

We shall never know for sure, but after that grand cotillion, Mr. Davis seemed to grow sullen and moody. No one took much notice, however, until a bitterly cold day some three weeks later. That morning, as he did every day, one of the employees climbed the stairs and knocked on the door of Room 13 to call the Davises to breakfast. There was no answer, which was odd because Mr. Davis was an early riser.

After knocking on the door and calling their names several times, the employee, a man named Roy, ventured to open the door, fearing that something was amiss. It was.

When Roy slowly opened the door, he was confronted by a scene of gore and horror unlike anything ever previously witnessed in the region. Still in bed, her fine white linen sheets stained crimson, Mrs. Davis lay dead, with her throat cut from ear to ear. Nearby, in a heap, was Mr. Davis, blood still oozing from a wound in his head. In shock, the terrified Roy stumbled down the stairs and ran to the house of the local physician, Dr. Raynes, for help.

Within minutes, the whole town was awakened and electrified by the news of the murders. After careful examination, Dr. Raynes and the authorities were able to piece together what had happened.

Davis had risen early and, for whatever reason, had gone into the bathroom, taken out his large straight razor, and sharpened it carefully on his barber's strop. He then returned to the bedroom and slashed his beautiful young wife to death in a most barbarous fashion. Dr. Raynes determined that Davis had taken some poison, but it apparently did not work quickly enough to suit the innkeeper, who subsequently loaded his derringer and shot himself in the head.

What had driven Davis to such a horrible deed? Was it jealousy? Depression? Madness? Or was it simply Room 13? We shall never know for sure, but this much is certain: Room 13, once considered unlucky, was now regarded with absolute dread. A pall fell over the whole hotel after the incident, and rumors began to spread that a malevolent presence was infesting the building.

When the second Tabard Inn caught fire a few years later, it was not regarded as an unmitigated tragedy. Curiously, Room 13 was the last room to be consumed by the blaze. Many who witnessed the conflagration swore that they heard a horrifying groan arise from Room 13 just before the entire structure collapsed into fiery rubble.

Today, nothing remains of the old Tabard Inn, save for its overgrown stone foundation. All that survives from the ill-fated hostelry are some pieces of furniture that were rescued from the flames—including the furniture from Room 13. Over the years, these pieces have found their way into nearly every house in town, including Newbury House—which also is haunted.

Like the original Tabard Inn at Rugby, Newbury House boasts a mansard roof and a verandah. Although built on a considerably more modest scale than the old Tabard, Newbury House plays host to the public as well, offering comfortable rooms to guests visiting Historic Rugby.

But the inn's quaint Victorian charm belies unseen and uninvited guests. On several occasions, guests at Newbury House have reported waking in the middle of the night to see the ghostly figure of a man standing over their bed. Two rooms of the otherwise cozy bed and breakfast seem peculiarly favored in this regard.

The ghost at Newbury House is reputed to be a certain Mr. Oldfield, who had been sent out to report on the fledgling colony in the 1880s. Oldfield took a liking to the place and sent for his wife and son from England. Tragically, Oldfield died of a heart attack at Newbury House the very night before his son arrived.

Many believe that Oldfield is still waiting for his son's arrival, but others claim that a more malevolent presence haunts Newbury House: the ghost of Davis, the Tabard's razor-wielding innkeeper, who roams from room to room. Several pieces of furniture from Room 13 have found their way to Newbury House over the years, and many feel that the disturbed spirit of Davis came with them. Of course, it could also be that both spirits abide within the walls of Newbury House. In Rugby, anything is possible.

Culture, of course, was very important to the English colonists of Rugby. A great deal of care was lavished on the community's library, now the Thomas Hughes Free Public Library. In a sense, that building embodies the spirit of Rugby—and many believe a disembodied librarian presides over it.

Rugby's first librarian was apparently a very meticulous and fussy fellow. He refused to allow any volume in the library to be taken out unless it had been properly catalogued first, and many say that the man also was somewhat persnickety about late returns.

It is believed that his protective spirit still lingers in the library, guarding his prized collection. Those who hold to this notion cite the fact that every single one of the library's original seven thousand volumes are still in place, in virtually the same pristine condition as when they were first placed on the shelves more than a century ago.

As a result, the library, which boasts one of the most complete collections of Victorian literature in existence, has been dubbed the "Rip Van Winkle Library." Walking into the building is like stepping back in time. Legend has it that if one visits the library at twilight, the phantom librarian's presence is almost tangible. He is, it seems, a quiet ghost—just so long as no one disturbs his precious collection of books.

Thomas Hughes had a house built in Rugby that he called Kingston Lisle, and it was to that house that he eventually planned to retire. While Hughes never did move permanently to Rugby, he stayed at Kingston Lisle whenever he came to look in on his beloved colony.

Hughes's once forlorn cottage is now believed to be home to a ghost as well. This phantom, it seems, is peculiar in that it neither walks nor floats, nor does it howl or rattle chains; it simply snores. Residents of the house have noticed the ghost most often while enjoying breakfast or having a spot of afternoon tea (still de rigueur for inhabitants of Rugby). The distant sound of snoring can be heard drifting through the rafters into the downstairs dining room.

In the 1960s Mr. and Mrs. Wickman, the owners at the time, had their home thoroughly examined by psychic experts, who determined that the snoring sounds were not the result of wind, plumbing, or any mechanical appliances. It is, quite simply, a spirit who has come Goldilocks-like to catch up on some lost slumber. The snoring ghost has even been known to kick the sheets off the neatly made upstairs beds from time to time.

The Wickmans came to regard their spectral boarder at Kingston Lisle as just another member of the household. They even missed him whenever he would fail to make his presence known in their home.

A ghost of a considerably more boisterous sort is the spirit that frequents Roslyn, a stately two-story home built in Rugby in 1886. Roslyn was once home to the founding director of Historic Rugby, Brian Staggs, who, after viewing the decaying splendor of old Rugby as a teenager, resolved to restore the village to its former glory. Staggs, at times almost single-handedly, rescued the architecture and heritage of this unique mountain community. Tragically, he died in 1976, while still in his late twenties—but not before he had helped rescue Rugby from the brink of extinction. Staggs's own piece of Distant Eden was Roslyn.

Mrs. Jesse Tyson and her children were Roslyn's first

residents, and she named the house after her family's ancestral castle in Scotland. In Mrs. Tyson's day, a circular driveway led up to the building, and her English gardener turned the grounds into a floral tapestry of shrubs and flowers. The Tysons were also fond of entertaining, and during its heyday, the house's large hall was often used as a ballroom for parties.

Modern researchers at Rugby have uncovered the fact that Mrs. Tyson's spirited son, Jesse, often drove a tally-ho carriage, drawn by a team of four horses and loaded with young people, to and from nearby Sedgemoor. He would race up and down the steep, rocky road and over the wooden toll bridge that at the time spanned the White Oak River.

Long before Brian Staggs bought and restored Roslyn, several visitors to the home had reported hearing the clatter of horses' hooves and carriage wheels. Some even said they had seen a black coach—pulled by four black horses and with a ghostly driver at the reins—racing up to the house.

The phantom carriage would thunder toward the building, turn in a circle before it, then race away at a gallop, disappearing into the thick forest nearby. In recent years, archaeologists have verified that a road called High Street did indeed lay along the route the phantom carriage follows. Could this be the joyriding Jesse? Many think it just may be.

The mad carriage driver is but one of several spirits that have been reported at Roslyn. When Brian Staggs first moved into the house, he quickly became aware of a supernatural presence within the walls as well. At first, there were minor incidents. When Staggs would go into the garden, for example, the door would lock itself behind him. Later, Staggs would be awakened in the night by footsteps in the hallway. Finally, he began to see an apparition of a lady in Victorian dress pacing the halls and sobbing.

An independent observer, Sarah Bonner, confirmed Staggs's sightings, claiming that she also had seen the sobbing lady. The spectral woman's features were so well defined that both Staggs and Bonner were able to identify her from old photographs—she was none other than Sophie Tyson, Jesse's only sister. Was she perhaps mourning over a lost love? Whatever the cause of her sadness, her restless spirit still resides within Roslyn.

On another occasion, three men—one a reporter—visited Staggs at Roslyn. While standing and talking in an upstairs bedroom, three of the four saw the image of a tall man in a black shroud who gave off a luminous glow while hovering in midair above the bed. Shrieking in terror, they made a beeline for the door!

As if all these spirited doings were not sufficiently spooky, there is some evidence to indicate that Rugby has had at least one resident witch as well.

Among the first families to settle in the community were the Riddells, well-to-do folk of English extraction who had moved to Rugby from Kentucky. The home they built was at one time simply called "the Mansion" because of its grandeur and size. Today, it is more commonly know as Twin Oaks, due to two massive black oak trees that flank the entrance to the house like looming sentinels.

While Twin Oaks cannot boast of ghosts like other homes in town, the Riddell family did at one time employ a local washerwoman named Matilda who, it seems, claimed to be a "wisewoman." In Colonial New England, Matilda likely would have been burned at the stake by townspeople, but in the South, persons claiming occult powers were often regarded with a mixture of awe and respect.

During frontier times especially, wisewomen and "herb doctors" were considered to be essential. They often were the only persons available to cure diseases, bind wounds, and remove hexes. Given the low priority placed on hygiene by the medical establishment of the day, these rural wisewomen probably were more effective healers than were their college-educated counterparts.

Fortunately for all concerned, Matilda was never

known to engage in malicious witchcraft, preferring instead to brew an herb tea for a cough or to concoct a poultice or a love potion. By far the most enchanting spells Matilda wove in the Riddell house were the tall tales she would recount on dark and stormy nights. By her own admission, Matilda was in personal contact with the supernatural—a feat that was not terribly difficult in ghost-laden Rugby. By the 1960s, however, the Riddells were long gone—and so too was Matilda. Today, only the memory of Twin Oaks' faded grandeur haunts the place.

In many ways, though, the ghosts of Rugby are much like old Matilda: essentially harmless and more a comfort than a terror. After all, it would be terribly bad manners for a proper English ghost to disturb its hosts too much.

Every year, tens of thousands of people tour historic sites such as Rugby to see the past come alive. At Rugby, however, those who visit for even a short while cannot avoid the feeling that, in a very real and tangible sense, remnants of the past still dwell among us.

2

THE LADY IN WHITE,
THE LADY IN BLACK—AND
THE HOUND FROM HELL

ROWENA WAS HER NAME, AND IT IS SAID
that, in her day, she was the fairest maiden, if not in all
Christendom, then certainly in all the Holston Valley.
There is little doubt that she was her father's greatest
joy—and his ultimate sorrow.

Rowena's father, the Reverend Frederick A. Ross,
was a man who always liked to think of himself as a Virginia Gentleman. A most enterprising fellow, it was he
who laid out the Tennessee town of Rossville—later
called Kingsport—and founded another community
named Christianville. In addition to founding towns,
building bridges, and ministering to his flock, the reverend also ran Rotherwood Plantation.

While his duties often kept him quite busy, the reverend still found time to read. Frederick Ross was particularly fond of the writings of Sir Walter Scott, so much
so, in fact, that he named Rotherwood after a locale in
Scott's epic romance *Ivanhoe* and his daughter after the
heroine of the same novel. Reverend Ross showered
Rowena with everything a father's money could buy, for
he doted on her and could deny her nothing.

In a short span of years, the flaxen-haired Rowena
grew from child to young woman. As talented as she was

24

beautiful, Rowena was educated in the finest Northern schools and was a skilled musician and charming hostess who was much sought after by the young gentlemen of Kingsport. She had been out of school for just a few years when a young man won her heart and persuaded her to marry him.

It so happened that on the day before their wedding, the groom went on a fishing trip on the Holston with some chums, promising to return in plenty of time for the nuptials. As their small boat drifted down the North Fork of the Holston toward Rotherwood—some say the craft had just come within sight of Rowena—it capsized in the river's unpredictable currents. Soon the desperate cries of drowning men echoed off the surrounding hills.

Reverend Ross's servants rushed to the men's assistance, as did everyone else within earshot, and all of the young men were rescued except one: Rowena's beloved. Rescue parties searched all that day and into the night, and when dawn came, they dragged the river once more. Finally, at the very hour the young couple was to have been wed, searchers recovered the groom's body. His bloated and discolored corpse was brought ashore near Rotherwood as beautiful Rowena looked on in horror.

Words cannot express the agony the young girl suffered in the weeks and months that followed. The outgoing, fun-loving Rowena became a semi-recluse, rarely venturing forth from the confines of Rotherwood. After two years, she finally emerged from her mourning and gradually began to socialize again. She met new people and seemed to have regained at least a part of her former joyous spirit. In time, Rowena married one of the many suitors eager for her hand, a rich man of good reputation from the Knoxville area.

For a while, it seemed that Rowena had regained her happiness. But before long, her new husband contracted yellow fever and died, and the beautiful young woman again entered a period of mourning.

Rowena eventually emerged from her grief, but it would be ten years before she could bring herself to accept the hand of another suitor. Her second marriage, to

Edward Temple of Alabama, produced a daughter, also named Rowena. But happiness once more proved elusive for the sad-eyed lady of the highlands.

After a long stay away from Rotherwood, Rowena returned to her father's house, the scene of her first tragedy many years before. Some say the plantation was already haunted—haunted by the spirit of her drowned lover, who called to her nightly; or perhaps it was simply that the sight of the mansion and its grounds brought back all of the painful memories to a woman already weary of this world.

Either way, one moonlit night, Rowena heard the call of the river. No one else heard it, but to Rowena, it was as clear as a siren's song. She climbed the wooden staircase to the upper floor and, opening a large leather and wood chest, drew out an old wedding dress—the gown in which she had planned to marry her first, best love.

Donning the white dress, Rowena descended the stairs once more, moving swiftly and silently, so as not to wake anyone. Forsaking her six year old daughter and all others who still loved her, Rowena strode quickly through the moonlit trees, making her way down the slope to the river.

Some say that from the banks of the Holston's North Fork, Rowena could see in the moonlight a pale gray hand beckoning to her from the middle of the river. Was it the wind in the trees or could she hear a voice gently whispering, "Come to me and be my love"?

As if in a trance, Rowena walked calmly into the water. Mountain streams run clear and cold, but that night the Holston felt warm and welcoming to the pale lady, as it first lapped at her ankles, then enclosed her milky white thighs, girdled her hips, encircled her breasts, and caressed her long flaxen hair. That was the end of Rowena Ross Temple—and the beginning of the legend of Rotherwood.

Not long after Rowena's death, neighbors and passers-by began to see a young woman, dressed all in white, wandering the banks of the Holston River near

Rotherwood Mansion. Many believe it is the spirit of Rowena searching the river bank for her lost love.

Jill Ellis, whose parents were caretakers at Rotherwood in the 1920s, remembers vividly the Lady in White. She recalls, for example, seeing the shade of Rowena sitting upstairs in a rocking chair, waiting for her lost love to arrive.

A doctor in Kingsport recalls a boyhood encounter with the specter while picking strawberries at Rotherwood. One day, as he knelt by a patch of berries, the Lady in White walked up and stood next to him. That was the last time he ventured onto the plantation grounds.

The Lady in White is not the only restless spirit wandering about Rotherwood. Frederick Ross, distraught over the loss of his only child, lost interest in worldly affairs. His numerous business interests began to falter and he fell into debt. In 1847, to pay Ross's debts, Rotherwood and over a thousand acres of land were sold to Joshua Phipps.

If the Reverend Ross was a goodly, godly man concerned with matters of the spirit and the mind, Joshua Phipps was a man wholly inclined in the opposite direction. Perhaps the most charitable thing that can be said about Phipps is that he was a man who had become lost in the dark night of the soul.

East Tennessee in the mid-nineteenth century generally was not a slave-holding region, and plantations such as Rotherwood were rare. Rotherwood had upwards of forty slaves in its heyday, a large number by East Tennessee standards but small by comparison to the great plantations of West Tennessee and Mississippi. Although slavery was a pernicious institution, the stereotype of the plantation owner as a sadistic monster was the exception and not the rule. Unfortunately, Joshua Phipps was one of the exceptions.

By all accounts, Phipps had a mean streak as wide as the Tennessee River and ten times as deep. Folks around Kingsport don't like to talk much about Phipps—and if they do, it is usually in hushed tones under the breath, as if they fear that he might hear what they are saying.

What horrors transpired at Rotherwood under Phipps's dominion remains a matter of morbid speculation, but they were real enough. The owner kept a whipping post in a room on the mansion's third floor, and there he would brutalize his slaves whenever he pleased. Their blood still stains the room's floorboards, and to this day it is said that when it rains, the stains return—as if the house cannot forget the cruelty it has witnessed.

People began to shun Rotherwood—small wonder, since agonized screams emanating from the upstairs whipping room occasionally could be heard echoing through the surrounding hills.

The malice of Joshua Phipps was proverbial, and his reputation for cruelty became part of the mansion's legend. Generations later, parents in the area still used his name as a kind of byword for the "boogeyman." "Don't go out after dark, or Joshua Phipps will get you," they would warn.

There seemed to be something unnatural about Phipps's cruelty, and the manner of his death and his subsequent burial only served to confirm area residents' beliefs that the house was infested by a wickedness of supernatural proportions.

From the fall of 1847 to the summer of 1861, Phipps continued to prosper, while his slaves endured his evil reign as best they could. But just before Tennessee and the rest of nation plunged into the massive bloodletting that was the American Civil War, Phipps fell deathly ill.

A black youth stood nearby gently fanning him and was witness to the man's last moments. As Phipps lay on his deathbed gasping for breath, swarms of flies materialized—seemingly out of nowhere—and made straight for the stricken man. More and more flies came into the room, landing on Phipps's face and crawling into his mouth and nostrils, until every orifice on his face was filled with the crawling, buzzing insects.

The black youth stood there paralyzed with horror, as the man choked and gasped for air through the obscene mass. Within minutes Phipps was dead. The Lord of the Flies had come to collect his own.

On July 10, 1861, hundreds gathered at Rotherwood Mansion to attend Phipps's funeral—more out of curiosity than sympathy, one suspects. Once the service was completed, the coffin was carried outside and placed in a horse-drawn wagon for the trip to the graveyard. Strangely, however, when the driver snapped the reins, the horses strained in their harnesses but could not budge the wagon. The sky began to darken, taking on a leaden and gloomy aspect.

After much effort, a stronger team of horses was brought out and hitched to the hearse. Again, the driver snapped his reins and cracked his whip, but the wagon moved only a few feet. A third team, consisting of large dray horses, was brought up and harnessed to the wagon, and with considerable difficulty managed to pull the hearse carrying Phipps up the hill toward the cemetery.

All the while, the sky became darker and darker, and it appeared that a terrible storm was brewing. As the black-draped casket approached its final destination, a flash of lightning split the heavens. An ominous rumble echoed across the valley, and a rush of bone-chilling, unnaturally cold air swept over the crowd.

At that exact moment, the black crepe draped over the coffin began to rustle. The crowd turned to watch in horror as a large black dog emerged from under the cloth and, once free of the hearse, raced up and over the hill. Everyone stood still, stunned into silent horror at the spectacle.

As the rain beat down on mourners and onlookers alike, Phipps's remains were quickly interred and those in attendance made their way home as quickly as they could. That night, everyone made sure that they locked their windows and bolted their doors. Since then, many in Kingsport have said that the very same Hound of Hell can be heard at night—especially on dark and stormy nights—as it wanders the grounds of Rotherwood and the nearby woods, baying eerily in the gloom.

A third ghost also haunts Rotherwood and is perhaps related to Phipps's malevolent spirit. Known as the

Lady in Black, this apparition, like the Lady in White, has been seen at various times wandering the plantation grounds. The Lady in Black is believed to be the ghost of a mulatto woman who was Phipps's mistress. It is said that the woman was even more malicious and evil than her lover, and that she grievously mistreated the estate's slaves.

The Lady in Black was done in by a mob of vengeful slaves who had had enough of her cruelty. Her screams, like those of her victims, resounded through the mansion as the mob savagely beat her to death. The slaves secretly buried her on the grounds of Rotherwood to escape punishment by civil authorities, and to this day, her grave site remains unknown.

In recent years, the old mansion has been restored and renovated, and it has had a number of owners. The last time the dwelling came on the market, in 1990, the real estate agent was well suited to handle the sale of such an unusual property—her name was Poe. Quoth the Raven—Nevermore!

3

HAUNTED HIGHWAYS

I WONDER AS I WANDER THE BYWAYS OF the Mid-South just what strange and wonderful stories the old roads could tell if only they could give voice to all the things they've seen.

Although old mansions seem to be a favorite abode of ghosts, the open road—especially in Appalachia—is equally favored by a number of apparitions. In the beginning, there were only the Indian trails, glorified rabbit traces, really. These trails pierced the forest gloom, winding, climbing, twisting, and turning in all directions. When the first white men came, they widened and improved the trails but generally left them intact. Later, these same rude trails became the wagon roads and stagecoach routes that led thousands west across the mountains—and into the heart of the Dark and Bloody Ground.

One of the most traveled—and most dangerous—of these routes was the Bristol Highway. Today it is just another peaceful and scenic country road, but during pioneer times, the Bristol Highway was a sort of "superhighway," and often the hunting ground of cutthroats and marauders.

Starting at Bristol, on the Tennessee-Virginia border, the road led by stages through Kingsport, Surgoinsville, Rogersville, and then to White's Station (Knoxville). From White's Station, another leg of the trail, the Cumberland Trace, led up and over yet another mountain range to the Valley of the Cumberland and Nashville.

Eventually, the route was extended all the way to the Mississippi River. Today, there are still stretches of the old two-lane blacktop labeled "Memphis-Bristol Highway."

In the late eighteenth and early nineteenth centuries, people headed west for many reasons. Some were veterans of the American Revolution seeking to claim their land grant; others were land speculators seeking to get rich quick; some were poor people who were down on their luck and hoping for a second chance out west; and still others were ne'er-do-wells looking for easy pickings on the frontier. In their own way, all were seeking a better life. Many succeeded, but more than a few ended their journey face down in a pool of blood beside the road.

Between the mud and the blood and the dark deeds, it is no wonder that stories of supernatural doings sprouted all along the old road's length. One of the most unusual tales that is still told today is that of Long Dog. Since the early 1800s, so many travelers along a certain stretch of the Bristol Highway have reported encountering Long Dog that there appears to be little doubt that the spectral hound does exist.

No ghost or demon, no matter how frightening its visage, could surpass the wickedness of the human monsters that infested the region's roads in pioneer days. One of the worst of these was a dapper cutthroat named John Murrell.

Murrell learned his trade early in life. His mother ran a roadside tavern, and she taught the lad how to relieve guests of their valuables while they slept. Murrell later graduated to horse-stealing and counterfeiting, and eventually mastered the trade of highwayman, with expertise in the arts of robbery and murder.

Once, according to local legend, Murrell and his band of ruffians were riding along the Bristol Highway toward Cocke County to spend some money they had just minted. A few miles outside of Surgoinsville, Murrell and his men came upon a family that had camped for the night under a large white oak tree. All of the family's worldly goods were loaded on an old wagon.

Not a group to pass up a chance for doing evil, Murrell and his men set upon the family, murdering husband, wife, and children. They even killed the loyal dog that had tried valiantly to defend the doomed family. After disposing of the bodies, Murrell and his brigands took the covered wagon and team of horses, and rode off into the night.

It was soon after this dark deed that Long Dog first appeared. He initially was seen beneath the white oak—now called Bugger Oak—on the very same spot where his master and family had been massacred. Long Dog's appearance is most peculiar. According to those who have seen him, he is as long as a split rail and seems to be surrounded by an eerie glow as he runs through the countryside.

Over the years, the canine apparition has seemed to enjoy playing with wagons on the road—trotting alongside them, pacing his speed to theirs, and even hopping onto an open tailgate. Yet when Long Dog reaches a certain point on the road, he suddenly vanishes.

Many are the travelers who have gotten the scare of their lives after passing Bugger Oak on the road between Surgoinsville and Kingsport. It didn't take long before that particular spot on the Bristol Highway gained an eerie reputation among the local folk. While many have avoided that stretch of road over the years, a few brave but foolhardy souls have actually made a point of seeking out Long Dog.

One such person was eighteen-year-old Marcus Hamblen, whose family lived near Bugger Oak. Marcus thought he knew the answers to everything, and being young, he also thought he would live forever. Marcus had heard all of the stories about Long Dog, and like many people, he regarded them as just so much stuff and nonsense. Marcus didn't hold with the notion of "haints"; he thought they were most likely some bluetick hound kicking up a little dust. "If that old hound ever chases me," Marcus thought, "I'll whop him upside the head and have done with him!"

One night, just as Marcus passed Bugger Oak while returning home by way of the Bristol Road, the great glowing hound suddenly appeared beneath the hoary tree. Not waiting for it to approach, Marcus grabbed a long piece of wood railing from a tumbledown fence where a stand of cedar trees now grows. Rushing over to the glowing beast, he swung the rail with all his might. Much to his surprise, the wooden beam passed right through the dog without harming him, and Marcus was thrown off balance.

When the young man regained his feet, he saw the dog was still there, grinning from ear to ear and with its luminous tongue hanging from its mouth. At that instant, Marcus realized that all the stories were true—there really was a phantom hound!

Marcus scrambled down the road, running for dear life. The trouble was that Long Dog took the youngster's mad dash as an invitation to race and began to run alongside him. After a goodly distance, an exhausted Marcus had to stop to catch his breath, dog or no dog. The ghostly canine halted as well.

As soon as he caught his breath, Marcus was off again, running at what he thought was a breakneck pace—until he saw Long Dog just loping along beside him, enjoying the brisk run. Finally, after Marcus had run a couple of miles down the Bristol Highway, Long Dog vanished just as mysteriously as he had appeared.

That was the last time Marcus Hamblen ever tried to kill Long Dog—but it wasn't the last time he saw the creature. After a time, Marcus and the other inhabitants of the area came to lose their fear of Long Dog. They eventually saw that the phantom hound meant no harm to anyone— he was simply standing guard under the old oak tree, waiting for the day his master would come back to fetch him. And for all I know, he's standing there still.

Up the old stagecoach road, near Blountville, sits the Sturm cabin. Built around 1771, the venerable log home has seen many a change of season.

When the cabin was new, it lay on the very edge of

the frontier. Revolution, Indian raids, civil uprisings—all these and more have flowed past its door, and it seems almost inevitable that some of the tumultuous events should have left an impression on the old building.

For some years now, the Sturm cabin reputedly has been haunted. Rumors of strange happenings had circulated throughout the area for quite some time, but no one ever claimed to have seen anything.

In 1972 a passer-by saw a man on horseback riding, riding, riding at a furious pace up the street to the cabin's door. His heavy gray cloak—long enough to cover the flanks of the horse—fluttered in the breeze behind him. The man was clean shaven, and his long brown hair was tied in queue at the base of his neck; on his head rested a weathered tricornered hat. He reined the horse to a stop and dismounted, revealing a pair of old fashioned stockings and knee-breeches, and raced to the cabin door.

The eyewitness might have mistaken the man for a modern-day historical reenactor, except for one thing: when the oddly dressed figure reached the cabin door, he began to climb steps that were no longer there! The horseman rose into the air—gaining the height of a doorstep with each stride—and when he reached the door, he vanished into thin air.

People who study such things say the Phantom Horseman of Sturm Cabin is a "psychic imprint," a ghostly image of a specific incident that occurred long ago. Much as one might replay a scene from a taped movie or television episode, this ghost seems to be replaying a moment he once experienced; the only difference is, this is real!

The old Memphis-Bristol Highway was long ago replaced by Interstate 40. One would think that a modern superhighway would not be troubled by spooks, boogeymen, or other preternatural things—but one would be wrong.

There is a particular stretch of I-40, the portion that crosses the Cumberland Mountains, that many say is haunted. Drivers passing through this area have reported being buzzed by eerily glowing balls of light—ghost lights.

According to residents of the region, an elderly miser's cabin once stood near the place where the Obed River crosses the interstate on its journey to the Cumberland. In those days, the area was a wilderness, and the man's nearest neighbors were miles away. Some young thugs apparently made the journey to the cabin with the intent of forcing the old miser to reveal where he had hidden his gold and then taking it from him.

The ne'er-do-wells tried to pry the secret of the hidden gold from the man, but he fought back and during the struggle, the cabin was set afire. The thugs never found the gold, and they died along with the miser in the conflagration. Many say that the restless souls of the three men haunt the spot to this day and that they rise from the ruins of the cabin as three glowing lights that dance about the hills and vales surrounding the Obed.

On occasion, motorists driving along this stretch of I-40 have seen the lights—and there are even reports that the lights sometimes have chased autos down the road.

Be they buffalo trail, coach road, or interstate, the highways and byways of East Tennessee have never seemed to lack for lore. Nearly every mountain, valley, and craggy defile has its own tale to tell. So, whether you're traveling major thoroughfare or back road, bear in mind that beyond the natural wonders are supernatural wonders as well.

4

WICKED WITCHES OF
THE EAST

*"For we wrestle not against flesh and blood but
against principalities, against powers, against
the rulers of the darkness of this world—against
spiritual wickedness in high places."*

—Paul to the Ephesians

IT HAS BECOME THE FASHION NOWADAYS
to think of witches as harmless mythical creatures. To
many, they are just wart-nosed old hags, good for a laugh
at Halloween. Obviously, people who hold such beliefs
have never spent much time in the backcountry of Appalachia.

Consider this: What if one of your neighbors—perhaps even one of your own relatives—were a witch, a
real witch, one that meant to do you harm? And what if
no one would believe you when you warned them about
it? Think it couldn't happen? Think again—it may already have.

Witchcraft in the Americas predates the arrival of
Columbus. There are ancient Mexican texts that show
witches flying about naked, much as they were believed
to have done in medieval Europe. Thousands of miles
apart, yet doing the same things—the sisterhood of
witches was a far-reaching one . . . and powerful, too.

More recently, during Colonial times, the town of Salem, Massachusetts, gained a measure of notoriety by trying a few of its residents for witchcraft and then executing them. Salem wasn't alone in its abhorrence of the occult; in fact, all the American colonies had laws against witchcraft. Some say that the reason one never hears about witch hunts in the South during the nation's early years is that southerners were so good at raising hell on their own they had no need to make a pact with the devil.

But the truth is that, in the realm of the Dark and Bloody Ground, witches and the fear of witches were facts of everyday life. There are even a few documented instances of people being brought up on charges of witchery.

Take the case of Joe Stout of Jamestown, Tennessee. When the posse came to arrest Joe for bewitching a young girl named Taylor, their guns were loaded with silver bullets. It seems the girl had taken sick with a strange malady and had blamed the illness on old man Stout.

Stout was put on display in the town stocks and denied food and water. Passers-by spat on him and hurled insults—and a few other things.

The townsfolk had good reason to believe that Joe Stout possessed occult powers. At his trial, witnesses testified that old Joe often stayed up till all hours pouring over arcane texts of magic and the occult. Others swore they saw the old man pass through keyholes to get through locked doors, and that he had uncanny powers over man and beast. Some expressed a desire to have Judge Lynch render a verdict; fortunately for Joe, they had to settle for a jury trial instead.

As it turned out, if the Salem witches had had Joe Stout's lawyer, it's more than likely they would have ended up owning the town. It seems the wily Mr. Stout had secured the services of one John Marshall Clemens— little Samuel Clemens's pappy.

This "devil's advocate" went right to work on the case, and before you knew it, he had a flurry of briefs and motions flying left and right—enough to bumfuzzle even the sharpest judge.

Right off, Clemens pointed out a minor flaw in the prosecution's case against his client: the laws making witchcraft a crime had been abolished way back during the American Revolution. That kind of took the wind out of things, and it was not long before old man Stout had turned the tables on his accusers and had them hauled into court on charges of assault and battery. He won that case as well.

Jamestown must have been a hotbed of witchcraft—either that or the people in Fentress County had the heebie-jeebies—for a few years later a couple was charged with practicing the black arts in the tiny town. Hiram and Marsha Milsap were accused of the most awful things by William Bledsoe and Robert McIlwain. Marsha in particular was accused of transforming good churchgoing folk into "liars, sorcerers, and robbers of hen roosts." Bledsoe and McIlwain claimed Marsha was able to turn herself "into a suitable mate for the masculine gender of the canine species, which she had fully tested by experiment."

The two accusers petitioned the court to do something. It did—it convicted Bledsoe and McIlwain of libel!

Farther east, higher up in the mountains, folks know better than to try to bring witches to trial. For one thing, no jail could hold them, and for another, the witches could always influence a judge and jury with their magic.

Of course, if you're on the lookout for witches, the question that naturally arises is, how do you actually know someone is a witch? And if the courts won't protect you from their malice, how can you defend yourself against their spells?

Years ago, in East Tennessee, almost everyone knew the various ways to tell if someone was involved in the craft—and what to do about it. One sure sign was if someone was continually trying to borrow something. If a witch could borrow three things from a person, that person would surely fall under the conjurer's spell.

Likewise, a witch will refuse to lend even a close friend or neighbor anything, for doing so would jeopardize her occult powers. That was most likely the reason behind Squad McGaha's refusal of her sister's request for apples.

The McGahas and several other families lived, in much the same manner as their ancestors before them, in that part of the Great Smoky Mountains that nowadays is a popular national park. And just about everybody was convinced that Squad was a witch.

Nance McGaha knew that her sister was a witch, and not a person to be trifled with, but she had a hankering for apples from her sister's orchard and would not be denied. She promised to return the favor when she came into some apples of her own, but Squad would hear none of it.

Nance was insistent, though, and went to their mother to enlist her help. The stubborn Squad refused even her mama's entreaties, and the older woman finally told Nance to gather the apples with or without her sister's consent.

So it was that Nance McGaha went to her sister's orchard and proceeded to gather a sackful of red, ripe apples. They were the sweetest and juiciest apples one could imagine, and after she had picked as many as her sack would hold, Nance started back toward the house.

As soon as she turned for home, Nance felt something tug at her dress. She looked about and saw that a pack of squirrels had formed a ring around her and were tugging on her long dress. With each passing minute, more and more squirrels gathered about her, until the field was filled with the little varmints.

Scared out of her wits, Nance dropped the bag of apples and broke into a run, racing for the protection of home. But no matter how fast she ran, the horde of squirrels seemed to be everywhere, clawing and pawing at her and her dress. Nance reached the threshold of her house, then keeled over, dead. No one defied Squad McGaha after that.

Others who have had encounters with the wicked witches of the East fared better than did poor Nance Mc-

Gaha—providing they knew the proper countermeasures to take.

Sprinkling a ring of salt around one's house—or a person's body—is one way to stop a witch. If a witch should try to cross the ring, she would shrivel up like an apple left in the root cellar too long.

Another good way to keep a witch at bay is to place a broom across the threshold of one's home, for no self-respecting witch would dare step over it. In the mountains, saying that a man and woman had "jumped the broom" was another way of proclaiming that they had gotten married. A broom laid across the doorway before a bride and groom first entered their new home was the best way to ensure that some jealous witch would not cast a spell to ruin their marital bliss.

Of course, if all else fails, draw a picture of the witch, nail it to the back of a door, and then drive a nail through the image's heart. Do this and the witch will surely curl up and die—you hope!

In recent decades, both the mountain country and its inhabitants have undergone many changes. Interstate highways, national parks, and droves of summertime tourists have all left their mark on the land and the people of East Tennessee. One would think that such things as witches and witchcraft would be only a quaint memory in today's world. One would be wrong.

Belief in the supernatural has diminished quite a bit, and the old ways, for the most part, have vanished forever. But the mist-shrouded mountains still hold untold secrets, and things that many people thought were long dead and buried are simply lying dormant—just biding their time.

In 1976, a certain elderly farmer—we'll call him Bill—brought a complaint in court against two of his neighbors. Bill claimed that they and other people had been harassing him and his family. The method of harassment? Witchery, of course.

There had been a series of minor incidents, but what prompted the legal action was the mutilation of Bill's prized cow. This was no ordinary piece of vandalism—someone had cut off the animal's tail, slit its throat, and left the poor beast for dead. It was clear to the farmer that it had been a ritual sacrifice, one aimed at putting a spell on his farm and family.

The elderly dirt farmer remained stone-faced and serious as he told his story to the judge. However, every so often from the back of the courtroom, there was a snicker or chuckle as the farmer spoke. The judge was not amused and dismissed the case outright.

Old Bill got mightily upset at that and began accusing the judge of collusion with the witches. Finding the farmer in contempt, the judge ordered him locked up in the county hospital for psychiatric evaluation.

It was common opinion in the county that the entire Johnson family was a bit odd, and few doubted that Bill was touched in the head. But the county doctors disagreed. After poking and prodding and asking reams of silly questions, the doctors released him. Their conclusion was that Bill was perfectly sane—ornery as hell, but perfectly sane.

The psychiatric experts did express the opinion that Bill Johnson was "150 years behind the times." Nobody took Bill's claims seriously, but nobody was able to give a satisfactory answer as to how or why his cow was ritually mutilated, either.

Nor could anyone offer a rational explanation when, in 1985, the Johnsons' mule was discovered with a broken leg and multiple cuts and slashes all over its body. Again, the mutilations had all the earmarks of some sort of ritual ceremony. The county sheriff dismissed it as a case of "vandalism by persons unknown." The Johnsons knew it was the witches at work.

The dirt-poor mountain family continued to be plagued by a series of unexplained—and terrifying—events. On one occasion, a large black dog squeezed through the gaps in the floorboards of their house while the Johnsons were eating supper. The Devil Dog—for that's what it appeared to be—stood as tall as a man and walked around the shack on two legs, brandishing a gun.

The demon hound fired a round at the family, the bullet barely missing son Ben before becoming lodged in the wood-burning stove. The weird beast then exited through a crack in the floor.

In 1986, a ball of blue light—what some observers call a "ghost light"—charged into the Johnsons' house like a mini-tornado. The strange, swirling mass of energy went on a rampage, wreaking havoc throughout the dwelling. At other times, balls of light of different colors have been spotted whizzing across the family's property.

From time to time, the Johnsons have also been visited by disembodied shadows that sometimes appear as a silhouette of a cat or a person. At first, these shades of Dark Matter appeared on the wall of the barn and seemed to be talking. Later, members of the family witnessed the specters "up in the air, rocking back and forth." It was by the profiles of these shadows that the Johnsons were able to identify which of their neighbors were bewitching them.

Numerous other mysterious incidents have occurred over the years, from objects levitating off tables to animals walking up the sides of a barn. The Johnsons even believed Uncle Gideon was bewitched to death.

Attacks of witchcraft generally have been attributed to the witch coveting something of the victim's: a prized cow, a desirable mate, or a bountiful crop. In the case of the Johnsons, at first glance there would seem to be little to covet. For generations, the family had barely eked out a meager living by growing corn, tobacco, and other crops on a narrow patch of land in an isolated hollow in the hills.

The Johnsons' problems began when they turned down several offers to sell their farm to a high-powered land company. The big-city developers had just completed an upscale resort-home development on the other side of the ridge and were hungrily eyeing the family's farm as a likely spot to expand their operation.

Even some local businesspeople privately conceded that the land company used high-pressure tactics to try to get the Johnsons to sell. There was a strong suspicion that they may have recruited some local good ol' boys to terrorize the family.

Certainly, there was no love loss between the Johnson clan and some of their neighbors. Whether the neighbors went so far as to employ witchcraft remains a point of debate. But even allowing for the Johnsons' embellishment of the situation, there is hard material evidence that they were being victimized by someone—or something.

It is always easier to believe that someone is crazy or lying than it is to accept the possibility that sinister supernatural forces are abroad in the land. Ironically, even as the old ways have faded and mountain folk have adopted a more modern outlook, many city dwellers have become entranced with assorted New Age fads—including what passes for witchcraft.

Fortunately, modern-day "wiccans" bear little resemblance to the real articles. Media hype to the contrary, the oldtime witches were not nice people. They believed they had made a pact with the forces of darkness and were never hesitant to use their powers to cause harm to others.

There is much more that could be said about the wicked witches of the East—but, then, perhaps I've said too much already.

5

THE FOGGY, FOGGY HUGH

ONE OF THE BEST-KNOWN GHOSTS OF the Tri-City area of East Tennessee is a spirit whose goal seems to be preventing others from sharing his unfortunate fate.

Most everybody in Kingsport has heard of Hugh Hamblen, and quite a few folks have even seen him. He is arguably the most widely observed ghost in the Appalachians, perhaps in the country. Workers at the large Eastman Kodak plant have often seen Hugh Hamblen driving down the old river road at the end of a shift, and travelers have frequently reported sighting him.

It all began one inclement evening long, long ago. The Netherland Inn Road in Kingsport runs right by the Holston River in an old part of town. Often, cold air from the mountains comes down to meet warm, moist air rising from the river, and the two mingle to form a thick gray mist.

On just such a night in November 1923, with the fog so thick at times that a person's hand could get lost before finding a pocket, the figure of a man was seen walking across the road and up the hill. Clad in a tan trench coat, white scarf, and fedora hat, he looked to be about forty-eight or so years of age. It was a bad night to be abroad, but he was braving the foul weather for a purpose.

The man was Hugh Hamblen, and he was hurrying to Riverview Hospital, where his son, Charlie, had been admitted after being seriously injured in an auto accident. As the concerned Hugh hurried through the thick, foggy dew, his thoughts no doubt dwelled on what had happened, and what a shame it was the way folks drove these days. People were always in too much of a hurry to get somewhere; they didn't pay attention to the rules of the road; they caroused and drank as they drove—no wonder bad things happened!

The accident in which Charlie was injured was a good case in point. Hugh's son was a good boy, but one of his friends had gotten a shiny new car and had collected several of his friends to celebrate. The youngsters went drinking and sporting, and were having a high old time until, as they were winding their way down dark and foggy Rogersville Pike, a dog darted out in front of the Model T. The driver swerved, losing control of the car and crashing into the concrete abutment of a large bridge.

When the boys were found and pulled out of the wrecked auto, two were already dead and the other three were critically injured. One of them died soon after being admitted to Riverview Hospital. Charlie survived, in a sense—although his life would never be quite the same.

Thoughts of his son no doubt filled Hugh Hamblen's mind as he stepped back into the fog after visiting hours were over. In those days, the hospital lay just up the hill from the Netherland Inn and the road that ran beside it, and as Hugh walked back down to where he had parked, the gray mist enveloped him like a shroud. Although he was deep in thought about Charlie's condition, Hugh checked to make sure the road was clear and, seeing nothing coming, began to cross toward his car.

Suddenly, from out of the thick river mist, a dark object with two glowing eyes appeared. Before Hugh could think, the black shape slammed into him, then both he and the object bounded recklessly down the embankment. The shape landed on him, pinning him down.

His life ebbing out into the cold gray mist all around him, the irony of the situation was lost on the unfortunate man in the overcoat. Out visiting someone injured in an auto accident, he himself became a victim of a reckless driver. The girl behind the wheel, it turned out, had never driven before in her life. She said the car just "got out from under control."

Hugh had been badly mangled by the accident—fortunately the hospital was only a few score yards away. Within minutes he was back in the hospital, this time as a patient. Hugh's chest had been caved in, his ribs ripped from the sternum and pierced the lungs. He lingered for two days in the hospital, finally dying of his injuries.

Some time later, on another dark foggy night, along that same deadly stretch of road, a motorist was speeding along, unconcerned, when from out of the fog he spotted a man in a trench coat, waving him down. The figure in the tan overcoat stepped out into the road waving his hand and grimacing, directly in the path of the oncoming car.

The driver slammed on his brakes, but it was too late. The car ran right into the stranger—or so the driver thought. When the motorist got out of the car to help the stricken pedestrian, he was mystified to find the victim was not on the ground—nor anywhere else to be found.

Since then, drivers have encountered a figure at that same spot many, many times. Whenever the weather is bad, or visibility is poor and the road hazardous, the lone figure of Hugh Hamblen haunts it still, clad in his long trench coat and fedora. Workers at the big Eastman Kodak plant are among the many who have seen Hugh. His appearance on the Netherland Inn Road is at times more reliable than the flashing yellow caution light.

Although Hugh is a most helpful and familiar apparition, he is by no means the only ghost that inhabits that stretch of waterfront. The old Netherland Inn, which dates back to Andrew Jackson's time, is also host to a resident ghost called Old Andy.

The ghost of Hugh Hamblen has attracted the attention of several professors at East Tennessee State University—a school that is no stranger to spooks. At the college's Center for Appalachian Studies, researchers make it their business to examine the local folklore—and the local "deathlore" as well. Of course, academics are not supposed to believe in such things, even if it is their chosen field of study. But hunting for haunted places in Appalachia is kind of like looking for snakes down a dark hole—expect to get bit.

One researcher—Professor B—just couldn't resist going to look for Hugh Hamblen in the foggy dew himself. He took to driving the Netherland Inn Road several years ago, choosing stormy or foggy nights in particular to cruise up and down the byway.

He never did catch sight of the dapper Mr. Hamblen—maybe he was too safe a driver and didn't require a warning—but he did encounter something else. Driving along the old waterfront road one night, the professor saw a car on the shoulder. It was a Model T Ford—a real antique—but no one seemed to be around. Thinking that someone might be sick or injured, the professor stopped to offer assistance. But as he approached the car, he realized it was not really there.

When he tried to touch the auto, his hand passed right through it. It had no more substance than the surrounding gray mist. Returning to his car, Professor B turned on its headlights and saw that the phantom flivver was still there. He then drove on—right through the ghost car.

No one, least of all the professor, has been able to explain this strange encounter. Could the automotive apparition be the car of the girl that killed Hugh Hamblen? Or was it perhaps the shade of the fatal Ford that Charlie's friends drove to their demise?

Another ETSU researcher, Nancy Acuff, has studied the phenomenon of Hugh Hamblen in some depth. She has compiled at least 120 separate documented sightings of his cautionary shade. Nancy is a believer, for not only are the eyewitnesses credible and the number of sightings impressive, but she has a personal connection to the roadside attraction. Professor Acuff's full name is Nancy Hamblen Acuff—and the phantom in question is her great-uncle Hugh.

So, should you travel the river road in Kingsport when it is shrouded by the foggy, foggy dew, be careful how you drive—for if the police don't stop you, old Hugh most assuredly will.

6

STALKING THE WOOLLY
BOOGER—AND OTHER
SHAGGY BEASTS

THE MOUNTAINS AND VALLEYS OF EAST
Tennessee have long been renowned for their abundance
of wildlife. The casual visitor may not realize just how
wild some of the region's wildlife really is.

Although man has hunted many species almost to
extinction, big game still abounds in the eastern back-
woods of the Volunteer State: deer, bear, even an occasional wolf. But reports of bigger—and stranger—game
have circulated for generations. Truth is, credible accounts of weird and terrifying creatures date back as far
as recorded history.

In the fall of 1777, for example, a solitary French trapper was staying in a wilderness cabin on a bluff overlooking the Cumberland River. One day, while hunting in the
woods, he encountered tracks. They looked human but
were larger—far larger—than that of any mortal man. The
next morning, the trapper awoke to an unearthly noise and
heard something big prowling about outside, trying to get
into the cabin. That was enough for the Frenchman; once
the beast was gone, he fled from the cabin with just the
clothes on his back, swam the river, and continued to press
through the dense woods until he reached the safety of the
French settlements on the Wabash.

Early historians attributed the lone trapper's encounter to a case of mistaken identity, saying that what the man had actually heard was two American long hunters passing by. Admittedly, one of the two Americans known to be in the region at the time was of uncommonly large size—and nicknamed Bigfoot, interestingly enough. But the Frenchman was an experienced woodsman and hunter, well able to tell the difference between two moccasin-clad hunters and a giant barefoot humanoid beast.

Since the French trapper sighted his monster in the Cumberland Basin in the eighteenth century, similar tales of giant hairy creatures have emanated from all corners of the Mid-South. A large number of sightings have been reported in East Tennessee, where accounts of large human-like beasts date almost from antiquity, and it is here that such reports have been most frequent in recent years.

Long before the white man came, the Cherokees roamed the virgin forest at will. They knew all of the woodland beasts; they hunted them, revered them, and—in some cases—feared them.

One such beast was the Ewah, which, according to Native American lore, was not so much an animal as a demon. The Ewah ranged throughout the heavily forested lands of the Dark and Bloody Ground but was known to lurk in the darkness near Cherokee villages, waiting to catch a lone hunter or someone going down to the creek for water. Lucky was the man or woman it killed outright, for the monster devoured souls as well as flesh.

Like the ancient Greek Gorgon, the Ewah's glance was believed to be fatal. If it caught someone unawares, it could steal his or her soul, leaving behind an empty shell of a human—living and breathing, to be sure, but a mindless, drooling husk. Only the wisest medicine man or beloved woman had enough magical power to confront such a fey creature.

Though whites may scoff at such tales, many Native

American cultures have taken them quite seriously for centuries. According to tribal lore, long before the white man came to the region, the bloodcurdling cries of these hairy monsters as they prowled close to the villages in search of the unwary could be heard by all. Remains of ancient villages often show that they were once surrounded by massive earthen walls and log stockades. Were these structures built simply to keep out raiding parties armed only with stone weapons, or were they so massively built to keep at bay the monstrous Ewah and his kith and kin?

So many dangers beset America's early pioneers that tales of monsters such as the Ewah did not attract much attention. But by the middle decades of the nineteenth century, there was an upsurge in sightings of a gigantic apelike creature—a creature that often exuded a corpselike stench.

When taken separately, it would be easy enough to ignore or explain away some of these sightings. Taken as a whole, however, the reports of encounters with such creatures are remarkably consistent over a wide range of time and places.

Although published references to giant humanoids date back at least to the 1820s, the first reliable accounts of a sighting occurred in 1851, when an apelike creature was reported roaming the Ozark Mountains in Arkansas.

In 1869, there was a similar sighting in western Missouri, near the Kansas border. The newspapers preferred to call it a "wildman" or "what is it"—the locals had already taken to calling it Old Sheff. In the summer of '69, for some reason, the creature had come down from the seclusion of the high country and bedeviled the local gentry. It approached cabins, tore up fences (presumably in its way), and terrorized women and children. Farmers were reluctant to shoot it as they were uncertain whether it was man or animal—even after observing it at close range.

In Appalachia, newspaper accounts from the mid-1800s are scarce, but the region's tradition of hairy ape-men can be traced at least to that period—if not earlier. The Smoky Mountains and neighboring areas, for example, have long been the abode of the beast called the Woolly Booger. (A "booger," it should be remembered, is a local term for any malevolent spirit or entity.)

The trouble is, over the years, newspaper editors and local officials have tended to treat reports by wild-eyed farmers and others as just so much moonshine—or they believed the rustics were just trying to pull the editor's leg with a "windy."

Take the case of the Whirling Whimpus. Years ago, in the logging camps of the upper Cumberland, lumberjacks claimed some sort of demonic beast was stalking them. According to the jacks, the bloodthirsty creature would lurk near the woodland trails that connected the camps and the cutting sites, waiting to grab any unwary man who walked by.

The beast was virtually invisible because it had the ability to whirl around like a top, spinning so fast that it almost could not be detected by the naked eye. The only warning one had was the telltale sound the creature made, a sound much like the uncanny whirring of a bullroarer when swung about the head.

If one were not careful, the Whirling Whimpus would come out of its whirl right beside the victim and, with its enormously sharp claws, literally rip a man to shreds in seconds, leaving behind only a bloody pulp.

At first blush, one might suspect this creature was not just mythical but perhaps the product of some lumberjack spending too much time watching old Warner Brothers cartoons on Saturday morning television. But one would be wrong. In fact, the first published reports of the Whirling Whimpus appeared in 1910, and tales of attacks by the strange beast go back long before then.

Despite its immense size, reports of this shaggy monster consistently emphasize how elusive it can be. It has not survived in the woodlands for centuries without learning how to avoid being seen by its enemies. And given the Woolly Booger's propensity for stealth, one could easily see how it might have gained a reputation for "invisibility."

In 1878, a "Wild Man of the Woods" was captured—some say allegedly captured—in East Tennessee and transported to Louisville, Kentucky, where it was put on exhibit. Looking back from this point in time, it is impossible to determine whether the creature was genuine or just another sideshow scam. It is also not known what became of the Wild Man's body, if it existed in the first place.

From the accumulated testimony, one pattern of behavior is clear: the Woolly Booger—Bigfoot, if you will—normally keeps to itself in the remote wooded uplands. But, for reasons yet unclear, it occasionally will venture into more developed areas, and it is at such times that reports of the creature have surfaced in the media.

One such incident occurred in 1959 in the northeastern corner of Knox County. A "somebody or something," as one newspaper cryptically described it, peered into the front window of Ed Taylor's house on the evening of September 23. Taylor, fearing for the lives of his two small children when he spotted the creature, grabbed his shotgun and ran to the front door to confront it. As Taylor burst onto the porch, the beast skedaddled into the dark.

Going across Claps Chapel Road to a neighbor's house, Taylor enlisted the help of John Rosenbaum. The two sat under a tree in Taylor's yard to see if the creature might come back. Sure enough, some time later, the two men heard a loud thumping noise and, running around the side of Taylor's house, saw something running toward the woods. It was huge and ran on two legs—but it was not human.

From about thirty feet away, Rosenbaum let loose with two rounds from his shotgun, but neither seemed to have any effect. When sheriff's deputies arrived, the creature was long gone, but two long scratches had been gouged into the hood of Taylor's car. Neighbors attested to the fact that the scratches had not been there that afternoon when Taylor had waxed his car.

The following night, the "monster" returned to Clapps Chapel Road in Knox County. Authorities received reports from a number of residents who claimed they had seen a creature eight to ten feet tall roaming the neighborhood, and again deputies were dispatched to the scene. However, a search of the area turned up no sign of the beast. The Woolly Booger had escaped once again.

As interesting as that case was, perhaps the best-documented case was an incident known as the Flintville Horror.

Nestled in the outlying hills of the Appalachians, Flintville was just another small East Tennessee town—until one day in the spring of 1976, when police received reports that a large furry creature had broken the antenna on a woman's car. Not only that, the beast had bounded onto the roof of the car and jumped up and down on it as the poor woman cowered in helpless terror on the floorboard.

The hairy biped was obviously trying to get at the woman but, unable to do so, finally gave up and went away. When the badly frightened woman gave her account to the newspapers, others in the community began to come forward to tell of their own encounters with the beast.

Flintville residents described the monster as being covered with hair, standing seven or eight feet tall, and emitting a loud, high-pitched screech or call. One elderly woman referred to the creature as Ole Woolly.

A local man said he had been chased through the woods by the beast, which all the while howled like an ape. The disappearance of many head of livestock around Flintville was attributed to Ole Woolly's predations.

Then, on the evening of April 26, four-year-old Gary Robertson was playing in the yard when his mother, Jenny, suddenly heard a scream. Running outside to see what was the matter, she immediately smelled an overwhelmingly rank and foul odor—much like that of a dead animal or skunk—and was nearly overcome with nausea as a result of the stink.

As she rounded the corner of the house, Jenny saw an eight-foot-tall man-like beast reach its long, hairy arms toward her son. Panic stricken, she quickly crossed the yard and grabbed her son, mere seconds before the monster reached him.

Running back inside, Jenny Robertson called a neighbor for help, then phoned the police. When she last saw the creature, its large black form was striding into the woods behind the house.

Within minutes, a group of men armed with an assortment of deer rifles and shotguns gathered to pursue the monster. Throughout the night of April 26, armed search teams combed the woods in search of Ole Woolly. Several times, posse members heard grunting and snorts coming from the undergrowth, and fired their weapons in that direction. With each volley, the beast emitted a high-pitched squeal and, enraged, threw rocks at the hunters before loping deeper into the bush.

The next day, police and other searchers were unable to find the beast's body but did discover huge footprints, measuring sixteen inches long, as well as clumps of hair, blood, and mucus. One Bigfoot researcher sent hair samples to four separate police labs for analysis, but none was able to match the hair to any known human type or animal species.

Since the infamous Flintville incident, there have been sightings of Ole Woolly and similar creatures on Monteagle Mountain in southeastern Tennessee; in Dickson, Sumner, and Stewart Counties in Middle Tennessee; and also in portions of southern and western Kentucky.

A few irate farmers and a handful of dedicated local researchers have been hot on the beast's trail for some years now, but the Woolly Booger—or Ole Woolly, Old Sheff, Bigfoot, Ewah, Sasquatch, or whatever else you may choose to call him—remains as elusive as ever.

7

HILL COUNTRY
WONDERMENTS:
THE GAINESBORO GHOST
AND OTHER MYSTERIES

NOWADAYS, IT SEEMS THAT PEOPLE ARE too busy with the mindless hustle-bustle of modern life to pay attention to the wonderments all about them. For those city folks who have been culturally deprived all their lives, a wonderment is a phenomenon that mystifies the mind and senses, something that occurs all on its own and which no one can say for certain is either natural or supernatural.

Wonderments generally are not important enough to make the newspapers, and since they cannot be explained—or explained away—the "experts" usually choose to ignore them. Naturally, people who live near these unusual occurrences often have an explanation, sometimes several, but whether they get to the truth of the matter any more than the scientists' technical babble-on is a matter of conjecture.

Although you don't hear much about them anymore, wonderments are still out there, if you've a mind to look for them. And, if the truth were known, there are areas of the Mid-South that have an abundance of them.

Take the hill country around Gainesboro, for example, where strange happenings have been reported on and off for a number of years. The strangest, perhaps, is what inhabitants of this Upper Cumberland region of East Tennessee call the Gainesboro Ghost. In truth, this phenomenon is not really a ghost, but then, nobody is really quite sure what it is. It just is.

There was a time, not long ago, when one could find scores of cars from a half-dozen counties parked in the evenings along the shoulder of Highway 85 near the Free State Bridge, filled with people who had come to listen for the "ghost." There had been a similar visitation some years before, and folks claimed the ghost had returned and taken up residence around Sheila's Bluff.

According to one account, the Gainesboro Ghost is the spirit of a black man who had been accused of murdering a white man around the turn of the century. He denied the charges, protesting his innocence, but was found guilty and hanged in Gainesboro's town square. Some say the man got a raw deal and deserved to go free, and that his spirit wanders the area seeking vindication for a crime he did not commit. Others claim the wonderment is a headless ghost—the specter of a man who was decapitated in a freak accident and roams the countryside in search of his lost cranium.

Theories aside, one thing is certain: Something strange dwells in the high bluffs overlooking the Free State Valley in Jackson County. Sounds can be heard in the dark, emanating from some place around the bend of the river. Depending on who's listening, whatever is making the sounds is either talking or wailing.

The sounds are clearly not an echo, since they have been known to come at regular intervals, every two minutes or so, a circumstance that has caused a few people to speculate that they are actually bird calls. However, a few old farmers who are familiar with all manner of animal cries deny this, saying that no known animal has ever made such noises. To other ears, the sound of the Gainesboro Ghost seems to be that of a woman crying out in agony, and at least one observer believes the sound is that of someone calling "help."

The late Elmer Hinton, once Tennessee's foremost purveyor of all things weird and wonderful, investigated the return of the Gainesboro Ghost. He drove out to Sheila's Bluff one evening to see for himself but was never able to get to the bottom of the mystery. Bird or bobcat, headless phantom or disembodied voice, no one can say for sure. But like old Elmer—and everyone else in Jackson County—I confess I am still bewildered.

Some four miles up the road from Sheila's Bluff, in nearby Smith County, there is a phenomenon that is equally as strange, if not stranger. The Kemp Hollow Light is a wonderment that can't be denied—or explained.

Kemp Hollow lies in the Difficult community, and the light—unlike the Gainesboro Ghost—never went away. By all accounts, it has been as much a part of the community as death, taxes, and double-coupon week for as long as anybody can remember. One elderly granny claims that her great-grandfather, Haywood Kemp, had seen the light and that it was already well known in Difficult even then.

It is not unusual for people to watch the light flitting through fields and hovering over the nearby Kemp graveyard at night. Its shifting patterns remind some observers of an old oil lantern—the kind used years ago by farmers when they went to the barn in the dark, early hours of the morning to tend to their livestock. The Kemp Hollow Light, however, appears to float in midair, with no on holding it.

Glowing entities such as the Kemp Hollow Light are often called ghost lights and are thought by some to be the visible manifestation of a deceased person's spirit. One time, when there was a corpse in Kemp Hollow, the light did not go away for a full thirty minutes—the longest it has ever been known to visit.

Of course, not everyone in Kemp Hollow thinks the luminosity is a ghost. When interviewed some years back, Mrs. Ayers, a longtime resident, didn't believe in ghosts and didn't think the light was one, either. She claimed to have seen the light a number of times, and others have reported seeing it hovering over her home on several occasions.

Unlike some other ghost lights, the Kemp Hollow Light has been a fairly regular visitor for so long that many people thereabouts have come to take it for granted. Perhaps that is why it is not nearly so well known as, say, the Chapel Hill Ghost Light or the Brown Mountain Lights of North Carolina.

The Kemp Hollow Light has never been known to harm anyone, and while it still has the power to create a sense of awe in those who witness it, it has never been a source of fear. In fact, there was a time when the highlight of area youngsters' parties would be when the light appeared and frolicked over the hills and fields.

Now, folks who have never sat on their front porch on a warm summer night and watched a ghost light cavort and dance in the dark might be tempted to dismiss the Kemp Hollow Light as fox fire (a luminous fungi), swamp gas, or some other natural occurrence. But the hundreds of people in Smith County who have seen it over the years know better. Granted, fox fire is wondrous in its own right, but anyone who has lived in the country a spell knows the difference between the two.

The Kemp Hollow Light is not the only wonderment in Smith County, not by any means. There was the time, for example, that Aunt Ada and a friend were sitting up with a neighbor's sick baby and saw the "handkerchief" spirits coming for the child—but that's another story.

8

The Checker Cab Ghost

Anyone who has ever driven the night shift can tell you—it's a whole other world out on the streets when the sun goes down.

No sooner do the last rays of daylight fade than assorted creatures of the night—four- and two-legged alike—stir themselves to roam the land. And sooner or later, a hack driver will see them all.

Driving a cab on the night shift is an odd mix of tedium and danger. Mostly, you just sit and hope you luck out with a good run. Often as not, you end up waiting on some drunk to pour himself off the barstool and stagger out to the cab. At other times, you find yourself headed for the bad part of town, not knowing whether some slimeball is waiting to blow you away for pocket change. Big city or small town, the names change, but the game remains the same.

About the only thing a night driver doesn't have to worry about is ghosts or other supernatural creatures. The flesh-and-blood ones he encounters are scary enough, and they're more dangerous. Once in a long while, though, something truly strange happens that even the most jaded taxi driver can't explain.

Some years back, in the East Tennessee community of Gap Creek, the drivers with the local Checker Cab company had just such an encounter. It has been awhile since the incident, but I'll wager that you can still find some who remember it—and who will swear to a man that it's the gospel truth.

In Gap Creek, Checker was the main cab company and had a reputation for safe and courteous drivers. One night, a Checker driver picked up a fare that took him far out of town. Nothing unusual about that, but as the cab rounded a certain curve, something happened. From out of nowhere, a man jumped onto the hood of the speeding vehicle.

A less skilled driver might have panicked and lost control of the taxi. But this driver—we'll call him Jack—stayed calm, and as soon as he rounded the sharp curve, he pulled to the side of the road and got out to see what he could do to help the man on the hood.

But as Jack emerged from the taxi, a strange thing happened: the man on the hood vanished! More than a little shaken, Jack got back into the cab, drove his fare to her destination, and then returned to Gap Creek, where he put the cab in the rack for the night.

The next day, when Jack told the other night drivers about what happened, no one would believe him. "He's telling us a big 'sandy,'" said some of his fellow hacks. "He fell off the wagon again," laughed others.

A few weeks passed, another driver picked up a late-night fare that took him along the same route where Jack had encountered the vanishing man. As the taxi came upon that same bend in the road, at just about the same time of night—two o'clock in the morning—a man with a desperate look in his eyes suddenly hopped onto the front of the rapidly moving Checker. The man hung on for dear life as the vehicle swung round the curve, but when the taxi reached a certain point in the road, he disappeared.

The next day, the man tried to tell the other drivers at the garage what had happened but was met with hoots of disbelief. Everyone scoffed at his story—everyone except Jack.

A few nights later, a third Checker driver was traveling on the same road at about 2 A.M. As he approached the sharp curve, the cabbie cracked a smile at his friends' feeble attempts to con him.

The amused smile quickly disappeared from his face when, from out of the darkness, a man hurled himself onto the hood of the taxi. And when the vehicle rounded the curve and reached the same spot in the road as the other cabs, the phantom once again disappeared without a trace.

After that, none of the cabbies found the story of the disappearing man to be amusing. If they were not totally convinced that the incidents were of supernatural origin, all were at least certain that something very unusual was going on.

Word of the strange doings on the mountain road seeped into the community. Some citizens were curious about the affair—curious enough to look into the matter more deeply. While checking the local records, they discovered that a murder had occurred a few years before on that same stretch of road.

It seems that a man was being chased by an enemy who was out to do him serious harm. The man ran as long and as hard as he could until, exhausted and out of breath, he finally reached the road and tried to flag down a passing car. The driver refused even to slow down, much less stop, and as the car's taillights disappeared around the bend, the man's pursuer caught up with him and brutally killed him.

Since that time, it seems that the restless spirit of the murdered man has been haunting the scene of his bloody demise. Perhaps he is reliving his last moments—or perhaps he is hoping to change the outcome of that fateful night.

9

THE LEGEND OF
BOOGER SWAMP

UP NORTH, ALONG TENNESSEE'S BORDER with Kentucky, the Cumberland River flows through the Highland Rim, rushing through mountain passes and narrow defiles. For as long as anyone can remember, this has always been a wild place—a place with mysteries and secrets so strange that even the local folk choose not to pry into them too deeply.

Many of the inhabitants of the hill country are descendants of Scotch-Irish settlers, a stubborn and independent lot who possess a strong sense of personal honor and pride. Like their forebears, whenever they or their kin are wronged or slighted, these hardy souls will seek "satisfaction" by any means necessary—even if they have to do so from beyond the grave.

One of the most notorious sites in the region is a place called Booger Swamp. Located near White Plains in Putnam County, the shadowy wetland has earned a sinister reputation over the years. Even today, Booger Swamp is regarded with a special dread and fear by those familiar with the area.

Insofar as anyone can remember, the strange tales associated with the area began sometime around the 1850s, when a popular preacher passed through Booger Swamp while riding his circuit. Even then, the swamp was not considered to be a particularly safe place, but the man of

God had the Good Book with him, and as long as his horse stayed on the path, he felt that he was adequately protected from harm.

The minister was riding along, unconcerned, when his horse started to become skittish, then came to a halt and refused to take another step forward. As the preacher sat there, trying to figure out what had gotten into his horse, a pale figure materialized on the path right before his eyes. It hovered in mid-air and seemed as though it wanted something. To the preacher, it appeared as though the apparition wanted to communicate, to talk to him or warn him about something—yet it didn't seem to know how.

Just when the circuit rider thought he might be able to determine what the pale figure wanted, his horse whinnied in panic and bolted, carrying the preacher away before the phantom was able to make itself understood.

Now, the preacher was an honest and straightforward man, and his integrity was unquestioned throughout the highlands—in fact, it was a source of pride and honor with him. Thus, he thought nothing of telling his superiors exactly what had happened to him in the swamp. But when the church officials got wind of his story, they took a such dim view of the whole incident that they demanded that the preacher retract his story.

The minister protested, saying that what he had told them was God's honest truth. He had not sought the encounter, but it did happen, and he saw no reason to change his story. Believing that it would be a sin to tell a lie just because the truth made his superiors uncomfortable, the preacher refused to recant.

His superiors accused him of heresy and a host of other foibles, and expelled him from the ministry and the church. The poor preacher remained bound by his honor to affirm what he had seen, and he went to his grave proclaiming the truth of his encounter with the spirit of Booger Swamp.

The unlucky minister may have been the first—but certainly not the last—to encounter strange things in the swamp. Young couples seeking a secluded place for romance often have sought out the solitude of the swamp, and more than a few of these have reported seeing strange sights and hearing weird sounds while walking along its paths. Hunters, too, have claimed that their hounds have fled the swamp, yelping in terror, after encountering something in its murky depths. Many travelers have come to shun the place, often riding miles out of their way just to avoid crossing it.

Numerous stories have emerged to explain the strange doings in Booger Swamp. One holds that the ghost which haunts the lowland is that of an Indian maiden whose lover failed to return from a hunt. She, in turn, died searching for her lost brave in the swamp—and some say she is searching for him still.

Another explanation is that the haunting is due to a wicked innkeeper. A tavern owner named Quarles kept an "ordinary" at White Plains. One day, Quarles off-handedly advised a traveler not to stay at a competing inn up the road—in a town with the unsavory name of Pukeover—as it was a dangerous place.

When the innkeeper at the ordinary in Pukeover heard of Quarles's remarks about his tavern, he took umbrage—with a vengeance. One day, while Quarles was riding along the path that wound through the swamp, the rival innkeeper ambushed and killed Quarles, then tossed the body into the quagmire to rot. Since then, according to legend, the restless shade of Quarles has haunted the swamp, hoping that someone will find his remains and lay them to rest at long last in hallowed ground.

Murder victims, lost loves, or restless shades—whatever the cause, Booger Swamp remains a place ill favored by man and God.

But Booger Swamp is not the only haunted place in Putnam County. Putnam is also home to the Buckner Witch. Though not nearly as famous as the Bell Witch, like that spirit, the Buckner Witch has singled out one particular family upon which to vent its unearthly wrath.

The Buckners have lived in the Monterey community for generations, and as far back as anyone can remember, the Buckner Witch has been around to give them grief. Over the years, various family members have had encounters with this harpy, which most have described as a small woman who always carries a satchel.

Family lore has it that, in 1875, a woman tried to come between Uncle Alec and Aunt Margaret Buckner. Margaret, it seems, did not take kindly to some hussy making time with her man and one day borrowed her husband's horse pistols and ventilated her jealousy by ventilating the alleged Jezebel with lead.

Aunt Margaret had committed a grave offense, and while the scarlet woman may have been dead, her angry spirit returned from the grave to exact her revenge. On one occasion, her shade came into Margaret's bedroom. Aunt Margaret grabbed her walking stick and took a swing at the unwelcome visitor, but since you can't kill a person twice, the stick passed right through the apparition.

Since Aunt Margaret's day, other family members have seen the Buckner Witch as well. Passers-by often see lights on in Margaret's old house in Sparta when no one is home. Thinking that the ghost lights may be a sign of buried treasure, some family members have even ransacked the old dwelling in search of loot—to no avail.

Love, death, revenge, and retribution—that's the stuff legends are made of in Booger Swamp and along the Highland Rim.

WEIRDNESS ALONG THE WARIOTO: STRANGE TALES OF THE CUMBERLAND VALLEY

10

THE DEVIL AND GENERAL JACKSON

MOST FOLKS HAVE HEARD OF DANIEL Webster's legendary bout with Old Scratch. However, considerably fewer may know about former President Andrew Jackson's brush with the powers of darkness, in the person of the Bell Witch of Tennessee.

Of all the strange things seen or heard beneath southern skies, certainly one of the strangest was the haunting and harassment of a righteous rural family by a creature they came to call the Bell Witch. Even today, the story of the Bell Witch remains one of the best known and most unusual cases of the supernatural in the South.

John Bell was the patriarch of the Bell clan, and he, like Andrew Jackson, originally hailed from North Carolina. By 1804, the lure of the frontier proved too strong for Bell to resist, so he and his family packed up their belongings and, with trusted family servant Dean driving the wagon, headed over the mountains and across the forest to the Cumberland. In those days, people looked upon the Cumberland Valley as a kind of promised land, a land of milk and honey where a man could make himself into just about anything he wanted to be.

The Bells settled in Robertson County, Tennessee, north of Nashville and close to the Kentucky border. John Bell purchased a thousand acres of prime farmland along the meandering Red River and built a comfortable six-room log house.

It took a lot of hard work to make the farm productive, and even if life was not completely idyllic, the Bells enjoyed a comfortable existence there. The land yielded good crops of tobacco, corn, and other produce, and Bell became active in the local community, growing into the role of a well-respected country squire.

An old Indian trail wound its way through the property, and here and there about the land rose ancient Indian burial mounds. No known tribe claimed these mounds, which were a source of mystery and wonderment to the Bell children. As time passed, the trail became an important link to civilization, first as a mail route and later as a road for the stagecoach running between Nashville and western Kentucky.

There were ten Bell children, with some already grown and out on their own. The younger children often explored the nearby burial mounds, bringing back arrowheads, stone tomahawks, and various odd and mysterious artifacts. There were some who said later that it was the Bell children's disturbance of these ancient grave sites that first awakened the Bell Witch's wrath.

Others, however, point to a nearby cave halfway down a cliff overlooking the Red River as the real source of the evil that befell the Bell family. It is commonly believed that the cave had once been the abode of a powerful medicine man who conducted secret ceremonies and practiced the black arts within its shadowy halls.

By all accounts, John Bell was a very pious man and, as far as his neighbors and friends were aware, had done nothing to warrant the malevolence that eventually was directed against him. He read the Bible and led his family in prayer three times each day. Bell was also active in the politics of the day, often making "stump" speeches on issues he felt strongly about.

John Bell was a substantial and well-respected member of the community by 1817, which is when the family's troubles with the supernatural began. Bell's son Richard would later observe that, even before the witch's first visitation, there had been indications that something strange was taking place on the farm.

At first, odd knocking sounds could be heard emanating from the house's doors and walls at night. Bell thought these were merely the work of some prankster. Soon, however, the knocking was accompanied by the sounds of scratching or gnawing, which Bell attributed to some nocturnal animal. There followed, however, weird occurrences on the farm which could not be so easily ignored.

One day, in late August, John Bell was walking through one of his fields, checking the progress of his crops. Suddenly, he came across a monstrous creature sitting between the rows of corn. It resembled a dog in some ways, but it was oddly different. It glowered at Bell with huge eyes like burning coals.

Alarmed, Bell reached for his gun and fired a shot at the creature. Seemingly unaffected by the blast, the apparition disappeared into the cornfield without a trace.

Bell was not the only person on the farm to sight such a creature. Like many well-to-do farmers of his day, Bell owned several slaves, including Dean, the family's best and most trusted retainer. A man skilled in the use of ax and maul who was said to be "worth two ordinary men in a forest clearing," Dean also encountered the entity.

Not long after the incident in the cornfield, Dean was walking along the old Indian trail one night to visit his wife, who was owned by another farmer, Alex Gunn. As he strode through the dark woodlands, Dean found his way blocked by the dog-like creature, which growled threateningly at him. Dean was not a man to be easily intimidated, and when it seemed the black beast would do him harm, Dean hurled his ax at it.

It was at this point Dean realized the beast was not of this world, for the ax passed cleanly through it, and where the creature had one head before, it now possessed two! The spectral dog took to hounding Dean during his nocturnal visits to his wife, but Dean emerged unscathed, perhaps because his wife had given him a "witch ball" she had prepared as a defense against the beast. It was later learned the Bell Witch had a pathological hatred of blacks.

The strange sounds in the night continued for some time after these incidents, but there was no further escalation. Family members said very little about the unusual occurrences, and not a word of what was happening was mentioned to outsiders. Even the younger Bell children remained virtually unaware that anything out of the ordinary was taking place.

A few days before Easter, the Bells' oldest daughter, Elizabeth, known as Betsy, was in the woods with the younger children, gathering blossoms for the upcoming Easter service. As she reached to break off a bough, an eerie voice suddenly said, "Betsy Bell, don't break a flower; if you do, you will pay for it."

Startled, Betsy turned to the sound of the voice. "I looked," she recalled later, "and twenty feet from me, across the wagon road running through the woods, I saw, as distinctly as I see you, a ghostly looking woman dressed in pale green, suspended from the limb of a huge red oak tree. She was holding on with both hands, and her frail figure swayed in midair."

Betsy hoped the woman was just a figment of her imagination—perhaps a daydream or hallucination—and turned her face away from the wraith-like figure. But when Betsy glanced back, the pallid creature was still there. Trying not to alarm the younger children, Betsy herded them back home and told her mother about the encounter.

In retrospect, the Bells realized that this visitation marked a dramatic change in the supernatural activities occurring on the farm. The nightly noises—previously confined to the exterior of the house—began to be heard in the children's bedrooms. Moreover, the sounds were joined by physical manifestations. Bedsheets were pulled off sleeping family members and furniture was overturned by unseen hands. Then, one Sunday night, the entity made itself known with a vengeance.

The children were asleep on the second floor, Elizabeth in her own room, the four boys sharing another. Richard had just drifted off into a "sweet doze" when he felt something begin to twist his hair and then suddenly jerk his head off the pillow. Richard felt as though his head was being torn off. Almost immediately, his brother Joel yelled out beside him. Then, Elizabeth began screaming next door; her hair also was being yanked with great violence by some unseen malevolent force.

After this, the entity was no longer content with simple noise-making and minor mischief, and began to regularly assault members of the family. At first, the Bells tried to keep the infernal infestation a secret. If they referred to it at all, they described it as, "our family trouble." But the supernatural manifestations escalated with such rapidity and violence that it soon became impossible to keep them secret.

It was not long before the entity began attacking visitors to the house as well, and the invisible harpy began following family members to other homes in the area. Friends and neighbors offered their assistance, but they were as baffled as the Bells by the supernatural events.

News of the strange doings on Red River quickly spread far and wide, and the Bells soon were playing host to a rapid succession of visitors. Many of these people sincerely came to help; some, however, were merely curiosity seekers. Most visitors attempted to communicate with the spirit to find what it wanted with the Bells. At first, such efforts were fruitless, but gradually the entity began to respond. It first communicated with a low whistling sound and later with a feeble and indistinct whisper. Finally, the whispering became fully audible and distinct, and in time, the family could not get the spirit to stop talking.

The entity adopted a female voice—although it could mimic just about anyone's voice to perfection. At one stage, it even adopted multiple personalities, the chief one of which called itself Black Dog and acted as leader. This clutch of demons would often argue loudly among themselves, their voices overlapping. Finally, the entity adopted the persona of Kate Batts's Witch—Kate for short.

The Bell Witch's idiosyncratic behavior struck many folks as being more human than ghostly. Some who heard rumors of Kate labeled the entire affair a hoax, but no one who actually witnessed the unusual activities on the Bell farm came away a skeptic. By all accounts, the Bells were honest people and not capable of perpetrating such deceit. Still, there was a succession of people whose curiosity led them to see for themselves whether the Bell Witch was real.

One man, in particular, had both the will and the skill to determine the truth: none other than Andrew Jackson. By 1820, Major General Andrew Jackson had already won national acclaim for his conquests on behalf of the United States and had set his sights on the nation's presidency. Nowadays, people tend to forget that Old Hickory started his political career as an attorney and was once appointed attorney general for the federal Southwest Territory, formerly the western district of North Carolina (now Tennessee), where he investigated and prosecuted criminal cases on the frontier. Jackson had earned a solid reputation for bringing culprits to justice, and if anyone could determine the truth about the Bell Witch, it was he.

There was also another side to America's future seventh president. Jackson was a member of an ancient and secret fraternal order, a brotherhood whose symbols and rituals were steeped in the occult. Who better to go up against Kate than someone who possessed esoteric knowledge and was skilled in criminal investigation?

It has been said of Jackson that he would brave the very harrows of Hell, if need be, to help a friend. It is known that John Bell Sr. was active in Tennessee politics and that his son John Jr. had served with Jackson in the war. This may have been Old Hickory's main motive for visiting the Bell farm—to help out an old friend and political supporter.

Jackson was also a man with insatiable curiosity, and it is likely that the reports of strange doings along Red River were simply too tempting for him to resist. Either way, Jackson was determined to see for himself just what was happening in Robertson County.

Now, Andrew Jackson was not a man to do anything in a small way. Thus, the general set about organizing his

expedition to see the Bell Witch much as he had organized his military campaigns. He gathered together a
group of volunteers—friends, acquaintances, and assorted hangers-on—then assembled the necessary tents,
bedding, victuals, and other goods, and procured a "four-
horse covered wagon" to haul it all in.

When Jackson at last rode out from the Hermitage,
his plantation near Nashville, it was at the head of a column of mounted men, escorting the wagon laden with
enough provisions for a week-long siege. If a ghost could
be defeated by generalship alone, surely the Bell Witch
was a goner.

Crossing the Cumberland by ferry, Jackson and company headed north, following the old buffalo trail along
Mansker's Creek, past Kasper Mansker's abandoned fort,
and then crossing the bridge over the creek where the
trail forked. Here, the general and his men followed the
left-hand path toward the town of Springfield, seat of
Robertson County. From there, Old Hickory and his men
turned west onto the Red River Road.

Jackson and his cadre of ghost hunters made steady
progress along the winding Indian trail, which had been
improved to handle wagons and stagecoaches, and were
rapidly closing in on their objective. But as they approached the Bell farm, the group was suddenly beset by
trouble. In the course of casual banter, one of Jackson's
party made an offhand remark slighting the "witch." No
sooner had he uttered the words than the wagon jolted to
an abrupt stop. The teamster whipped and whooped at
the horses, but it was no use. The wagon would not move.

The sky was clear and the weather dry, and the road
was smooth and hard, so there was no earthly reason for
the wagon to have become stuck. Jackson dismounted his
steed and walked over to inspect the wagon's wheels and
axles. He looked it over from front to back, but neither
Jackson nor any of his companions could find anything
amiss. Even though the wagon was on level ground, its
wheels simply would not budge.

After the general had thoroughly inspected the
wagon, the drover once more cracked his whip—again to

no avail. After contemplating the situation, out of the blue Jackson exclaimed, "It's the Witch!"

No sooner had these words escaped his lips than a sharp metallic voice rang out eerily from the bushes beside the road: "All right, General," it said, "let the wagon move on. I will see you again tonight!" And with that, the wagon jerked forward.

The mounted party covered the remaining distance quickly and soon reached the Bell house. Seeing the group arrive, John Bell came out of the house and gave his old friend a warm welcome, then invited the entire party inside. Over dinner that evening, Bell regaled Jackson and his companions with stories of the days when Indians inhabited the land, of the mounds and mound builders, and of the mysterious caverns beneath their feet.

As the evening progressed, one of Jackson's party declared that he was a "witch tamer" and boasted that no spirit would dare expose itself while he was present. After the guests had supped, they went on to experience spirits of the liquid sort—holding quite a séance with them, in fact—and these spirits bolstered their courage for their showdown with the witch.

The witch tamer was a brawny man, with long hair, high cheekbones, a hawk-bill nose, and fiery eyes. Quite full of liquid courage—and of himself—the man let it be known that he had a horse pistol loaded with a silver bullet and was eager to try it on the witch. Braggarts can be amusing for a time, but even clowns become tiresome after awhile, and it was no different with the witch tamer.

At last, the boastful ghost-buster out and out dared the witch to do battle with him, but despite this bold challenge, the entity was nowhere in evidence. Jackson was becoming impatient and once more began to doubt the witch's existence. Leaning toward the man next to him, he said, "Sam, by the Eternal I do wish the thing would come. I want to see that fellow run!"

Presently, there was a lull in the conversation and perfect silence reigned. Suddenly, a sound like dainty footsteps could be heard on the floor, followed by the same metallic voice the men had heard when the wagon became stuck. "All right, General, I am on hand—ready for business!" it said.

At that, the witch tamer jumped up with a shout and began grabbing the seat of his pants. "Boys, I'm being stuck by a thousand pins!" the man yelled as he wildly jerked and pranced about the room.

The disembodied voice spoke again, challenging the witch tamer: "I am in front of you—shoot!"

The man drew his big flintlock pistol , cocked it, and tried to fire in the direction of the voice, but the powder in the flashpan would not ignite. Twice more, the witch tamer cocked and snapped the pistol—and twice more it failed to go off.

At each attempt, the witch taunted the man, urging him to shoot. Then, when it became obvious that it had bewitched the weapon, the entity exclaimed, "It's my night for fun!"

The next thing everyone heard was the sound of re-peated slapping—whack, whack, whack! As the visitors watched, the witch tamer reeled around the room as if he were being struck repeatedly by the unseen assailant. He tumbled over like lightning had struck him, and getting up again, started to caper about the room like a fright-ened steer, crying out in pain, "It's pulling my nose off! Oh Lordy, it's got me! My nose, oh my nose!"

By this time, the self-proclaimed witch tamer had had quite enough and made a break for the door. The oak door flew open of its own accord, and the man bounded outside, still seeming to be yanked about by something unseen. Once clear of the porch, the poor fellow ran full speed toward the wagon, howling in pain with every step. All the while, even as the man sought to escape his tormentor, the witch called out sarcastic advice on how to tame witches.

General Jackson roared with laughter at the specta-cle. "By the Eternal!" he told Bell, "I have never seen or heard anything quite so funny or mysterious in all my life."

Jackson asked Bell if he might stay the week to get to the bottom of the mystery—and no doubt enjoy more of the witch's antics. Bell gladly agreed, for even if Jackson could not free him from the infernal attentions of the witch, at least the visitors would distract the spirit from tormenting Bell and his family.

Once the pandemonium had died down, the witch spoke again, saying, "There's another fraud in your party, General. I'll get him tomorrow night. It is getting late, go to bed."

The Bell Witch assaulted no one else that night, but its parting words were apparently quite disturbing to many in the party. The witch had a reputation for knowing people's darkest secrets, even to the point of reciting their most private conversations. Few in the group were able to sleep that night, thinking of what the witch had in store for them on the morrow. As for Old Hickory, he was looking forward to a repeat performance—curious to see what the witch would do next.

By daybreak, the mood among the visitors had changed markedly. Almost to a man, they wished to be gone from the farm. Jackson, telling them he was sure the witch would show up the other fraud that evening, was keen to stay. But that comment only made his companions all the more eager to depart. They were, in fact, on the verge of panic, and there was simply no reasoning with them.

It is a wise leader who knows the limits of his men. Jackson realized that, at least in this instance, the better part of valor was a discreet withdrawal. By noon, the group had reached Springfield, and by the following day, the men were once again in Nashville. None of them ever returned to the house on the Red River.

Jackson's associates in Nashville were surprised to see him back so soon and plied him with questions about his encounter with the witch.

To this flurry of inquiries, Jackson simply replied, "By the Eternal! I saw nothing, but I heard enough to convince me that I would rather fight the British than deal with this torment they call the Bell Witch!"

11

SEASON OF THE WITCH:
EXPLORING
BELL WITCH CAVE

THE BELL WITCH TORMENTED POOR JOHN
Bell for three years before it finally drove him to an early
grave. With Bell's passing in 1820, the infernal proceedings on the family farm diminished. But neither the
witch nor the controversy surrounding what happened
there has ever really faded away.

The entity that haunted John Bell disappeared for
seven years after his death. In 1828, the witch appeared
again to certain members of the Bell family. Having
achieved its original goal of murdering the family patriarch, the entity exhibited an almost benevolent de-
meanor on its return, especially when it came to John
Bell's widow, Lucy.

But with the passing of Lucy Bell, and the dispersion
of the family, the Bell Witch seemingly disappeared from
the scene for good. Although family lore maintained that
the witch would come back again after a certain span of
years and haunt the Bell descendants, that was not expected to occur until sometime in the distant future.

However, the truth of the matter is that, from Lucy
Bell's death until the present, the Bell farm and surrounding Robertson County have remained a hotbed of
weird and unexplainable events. These events generally

have been attributed to the continuing presence of the infamous Bell Witch.

Since the Bell homestead was torn down many years ago, the main focus of supernatural happenings in the area has seemed to center around the nearby Bell Witch Cave. Overlooking the rambling Red River from atop the Highland Rim in northwestern Robertson County, the cave is near present-day Adams, Tennessee, and—by modern modes of transport—just a short drive north of Nashville.

In attempting to sort out the truth about the Bell Witch and unravel the mystery of the Bell Witch Cave, I and my small clan resolved to visit the cave and see for ourselves what all the mystery was about. Forsaking the interstate highways, we chose our route to follow the same path Andrew Jackson took on his pilgrimage to the site.

Where buffalo once roamed and Indians hunted, pickup trucks and automobiles now speed back and forth. Leaving Nashville by way of the Dickerson Pike— once a part of the old Kentucky Trace—we headed northward through Goodlettsville, where the venerable Dutchman, Colonel Mansker, had his fort.

Passing the old stone bridge that once spanned the creek there, we moved rapidly up the Springfield Highway—no longer the narrow twisting trail of Jackson's day but now a broad boulevard leading straight into Robertson County's seat. Ascending the Highland Rim from the Cumberland Basin, it was a short hop to the town of Springfield.

Like Old Hickory, we stopped at Springfield for refreshment and then turned our wagon westward. Once out of the sleepy little community, we were quickly surrounded by rolling hills and verdant pastures. Here and there, herds of cattle lolled about, sunning themselves in the slanting amber rays of early autumn.

The bucolic sameness was sporadically relieved by landmarks: a sign marking the site of Crockett's fort, another commemorating the Moses Renfroe party's defeat at the hands of marauding Indians, and the occasional ancient barn on the verge of collapse. After a time, the road narrowed and began to twist in and out among the hills, and colonnades of trees lining both sides of the curving country lane stretched their limbs to form a leafy arch above us. The sweet smell of burning hickory crept from between the weathered boards of tobacco barns that dot the region, and we could smell the aroma of curing tobacco wafting through the countryside for miles.

Arriving in Adams, we climbed out of the car to stretch our legs and ask directions to the Bell Witch Cave. The quiet village sits near the county line and the has recently begun to suffer the effects of modernization. For most residents, I guess, it can't happen fast enough, and as the graceful old buildings of brick and stone are torn down, flimsy glass and steel fast-food stores are hastily thrown up around town.

Adams boasts its own down-home variety show, the Bell Witch Opry, where visitors can still hear country music the way it used to be—before it went uptown. This Opry may be a little rough around the edges for some— but while it may not be grand, it is certainly authentic.

In general, though, there is little about the town of Adams to hint that it harbors one of the great mysteries of the South. Most of the community's residents are more focused on the future than on the past, and many are simply loath to discuss anything that smacks of the supernatural. Some people refuse to acknowledge the Bell Witch's existence on religious grounds, perhaps thinking that to recognize its presence in their midst would be akin to paying homage to the devil. Others may not speak of the entity for fear of being ridiculed if they were to admit to having a paranormal experience.

After obtaining directions at the local service station, we made our way the short distance to the Bell Witch property. At first, I thought I had misunderstood the directions; there was no sign to speak of, just a dirt track leading onto the property. But after bumping along for a few moments, I saw a modern ranch-style brick house sitting just off an aged sunken road.

At first, it appeared that the only inhabitant was a

large, ominous-looking black dog. My wife thought him cute, but then, she would have thought Attila the Hun was cute if he had four legs and fur. To me, it seemed the animal was eyeing us with evil intent.

A young lady soon came out of the house to greet us. She was the daughter of the present owners of the farm and cave. The cave had been closed to the public for the past few years, but the woman's parents, who bought the land from one Bims Eden, had made improvements to the grounds and reopened the cave for tours.

I arranged a tour for our little group in short order, and as we strolled north toward the riverbank, our guide gave us a brief summary of the haunting of the Bell family by the mischievous—and at times vengeful—spirit in the early 1800s.

Although the ghost (or witch or demon—take your pick) is supposed to have left for good in 1828, our host recounted a number of more recent incidents around the farm that would indicate something supernatural still resides there.

We crossed over an abandoned road, now merely a grassy depression in a hillside meadow. This was the road Andrew Jackson traveled when he came to visit John Bell Sr. Just east of the modern farmhouse, over a rise in the ground, the modern dirt road links up with the old trace, and a segment of the old Nashville-Clarksville trail now serves as an access road for farm equipment. It was along this stretch that Jackson's wagon became mysteriously stuck on his journey to the visit Bell family.

It was also along this path that Dean had his dark encounters with the witch in the form of a devil hound. Even today, the road remains the focus for a number of strange and uncanny incidents.

After a short walk, we came to the abrupt edge of a bluff overlooking the Red River. Climbing down the trail that hugged the bluff face, we had the strange sensation that someone was staring at us. The morning mist had lifted and a bright autumn sun shone down on empty meadows, but neither my wife nor I could shake a feeling of being observed. As we continued our descent, our feelings of apprehension and tension increased.

When we reached the mouth of the cavern, our guide told us more about the Bell Witch Cave. The original hauntings primarily had centered around the Bell family and their home—the caverns below them, though known at the time, received scant attention.

One odd thing our guide mentioned was that visitors almost always had a hard time taking pictures of the cave's mouth. Their photos generally came out cloudy—as if the film had been exposed to some unseen energy source emanating from the opening.

Following closely on our guide's heels, we entered the cave mouth and were quickly plunged into darkness. The cave is situated perpendicular to the riverbank and runs southwestward in a more or less straight line. The passageway was quite narrow at first, and a small spring-fed brook was nestled beside the footpath, facts that were revealed when our guide flipped on an electric lighting system.

A short distance inside, a passageway opened in the ceiling, but the cave's upper level was off limits as it was far too hazardous for amateur spelunkers to negotiate. This was the same passageway where one of Betsy Bell's companions once had a run-in with the Bell Witch .

The boy had become stuck in a narrow side passage, his candle had gone out, and he was wedged so tightly that no one could get a grip on him. Suddenly, the cave lit up like birthday cake, and a disembodied voice called to the boy, "I'll get you out." Sure enough, the lad's legs were seized roughly—as if by a pair of strong hands—and he was yanked through the mud and gravel until he was able to see the light at the cave's mouth. In this instance, the Bell Witch had been helpful.

With this in mind, and recalling that, as far back as John Bell's time, local residents had reported hearing the witch's voice coming from the river or the nearby cave, we continued our descent. After penetrating about 125 feet into the cave, the narrow hallway widened into a broad room. In this front room, on one of the upper shoulders of the floor, we saw an ancient grave, flanked by columns of stalactites. At some time in the distant past, a Native American had been laid out here in a shallow grave carved from the living rock and then lined with limestone slabs, as was the custom in this country once. The bones remain in place—no thanks to modern man.

Archaeologists had inspected the stone-box grave and left it intact, but other, uninvited visitors did not. Trespassers had tried to make off with artifacts from the grave. According to local informants, each person who removed an object from the cave suffered a series of misfortunes and physical injuries within days of the theft. The stone relics were returned to the cave, and no sooner were they back with their rightful owner than the "accidents" abruptly ceased.

It is commonly believed hereabouts that it is bad luck to remove anything at all from the cave. Our guide related a personal experience in this regard that had occurred about a year prior. While she was exploring the cave, she had come across a small and interesting rock on the floor, picked it up, and took it home as a good-luck charm. She knew of the taboo about removing anything from the cave but did not take it seriously. Just one week later, the family's tobacco barn collapsed without warning, ruining more than half their tobacco crop. While a cynic might say this was mere coincidence, our guide said she knew the two incidents were related. It was her belief that the barn's destruction was the Bell Witch's way of reminding the family that, while they may own the land, the witch still *possessed* it.

There are those who believe that this Native American grave is actually the grave of the Bell Witch and that the witch is really the disturbed spirit of an ancient medicine man or beloved woman. According to this theory, John Bell or one of his family had, by disturbing the grave, awakened the witch and incurred its wrath. Others, citing occurrences elsewhere on the farm, are of the opinion that the real resting place of the occult entity lies much farther back in the cave, in a remote chamber now sealed off to intruders.

Needless to say, our party treated the stone-box grave with respect, being careful not even to disturb the dust around it.

As we moved beyond this first chamber, the cave narrowed again, constricting ever more tightly, and old rockfalls slowed our progress. After some two hundred feet the cave opened into another chamber, smaller than the first, and in this back room we could hear the sound of water running clean and true. Beyond this room, the cave narrowed once again, leading to a substantial rockfall that barred further exploration. Miniature waterfalls and a shallow pool of water gave this part of the cave an almost fairyland aspect. It would not have been hard to imagine small sprites and elves frolicking in the small pond.

As we worked our way back to the cave mouth, it became obvious that there was quite a bit more to the Bell Witch Cave. How much more remained hidden in its depths was impossible to guess. The Bell Witch Cave has kept its secrets well.

Back on the surface, our guide revealed one more spot to us. On the other side of her home, beyond a dirt access road, stood a tall and rather ominous-looking grove of trees. Just inside the dark woods, one tree loomed bigger than the rest, a monumental oak rooted at the very edge of a large sinkhole. The tree's massive girth and height were further emphasized by the depth of the depression it bordered on. Some time long ago, the underground cave system beneath it had collapsed, creating the conical declivity. There was something truly eerie about the site.

As we approached the tree, the air became still and cold, and we noticed that there were no birds singing, even though they had been warbling gaily elsewhere throughout the day. It seemed as if all living things were avoiding a place of dread.

Our guide then told us that the oak and sinkhole had been the focus of almost as many supernatural events as had occurred in the cave. Once such instance involved a headless man who appeared to be walking through the woods en route from town to the farm. When the phantom drew near the oak, he would disappear. The apparition appeared regularly for many years, but when the connecting woods were cleared to make way for roads and new homes, the nocturnal visits ceased.

The oak and nearby road have also been associated with numerous sightings of ghost lights. Some years back, a previous owner of the property is said to have seen a lantern-like light rise from the edge of the bluff and float high in the air, finally coming to rest in the top of the oak tree. This happened each night for quite some time, until the man decided to put a halt to the unearthly proceedings and shot the light with his rifle. As soon as he pulled the trigger, light cascaded down through the branches and disappeared into the undergrowth.

The man and his family searched all around the base of the tree but found nothing. The light was not seen for some time after that—perhaps it was wary of the farmer's weapon—but it eventually returned to its old antics.

Bims Eden, the previous owner of the farm and cave, had quite a few run-ins with ghost lights throughout the 1960s and 1970s. There are some who theorize that the sinkhole marks the spot underground where the Bell Witch still resides. The witch, they say, never really left the land, as it had led the Bells to believe; it merely went into hibernation, awaiting the right summons to bring it to full wakefulness.

Although I cannot say how much truth may be in such notions, I can testify to the uncanny feeling I got as I stood by the sinkhole. The depression—a Devil's Hole—radiated a most unnatural chill on the warm and sunny day we visited. It is not beyond the realm of possibility that this "cold spot" marks the center of a supernatural phenomenon, a nexus from which ghostly malevolence emanates.

The sun was moving low on the horizon, and since we really had no desire to stay after dark, we thanked our guide for her tour and bid her adieu. Our old Chrysler jostled its way back out the dusty drive, but as we neared the gate, I began to think that we might not make good our escape from the Bell Witch's realm. There was the black dog again, looking even less friendly than before as it watched us with those burning-coal eyes. I was glad we were safely inside the car, and I made sure everyone's window was rolled up, just in case it decided to attack.

I commented to my wife again about the owner's black dog and how menacing it seemed. But she corrected me; she had learned that the family had one dog— a small brown lap-dog that we had noticed sleeping on the porch as we walked toward the riverbank. This was a much friendlier animal by far than the midnight mutt lurking near the gate.

My wife said our guide had told her that the black dog first appeared shortly after her family moved onto the property. The animal had not seemed to be lost or a stray; it acted as though it owned the place and seemed to take a personal interest in all the comings and goings on the farm. I looked at the dog as we drove through the gate, and it glowered back but did not prevent our leaving. I was relieved.

It wasn't until some time later, as I was delving deeper into the history of the Bell Witch haunting, that I discovered that the mysterious spirit which had hounded the Bells had originally taken the form of a large black dog and even called himself Black Dog at one point.

A coincidence? Perhaps. Our little expedition discovered nothing new, and the mystery of the Bell Witch is certainly no closer to being solved than it was before. But as Old Hickory told his cronies sitting 'round the courthouse square on his return to Nashville, "I saw nothing, but I heard enough to convince me."

12

THE HOMECOMING

"General Hood has betrayed us.... The wails and cries of widows and orphans made at Franklin ... will heat up the fires of the bottomless pit to burn the soul of Gen. J. B. Hood for Murdering their husbands and fathers.... It can't be anything else but cold-blooded murder."

—Captain Foster, Twenty-fourth Texas Cavalry

HOMECOMING OUGHT TO BE A JOYOUS and memorable affair. When Tod Carter came home late one November, it was most certainly memorable—though it was anything but joyous.

Theodoric (Tod) Carter had been away at war, defending the land of his birth. He had vowed, it is said, that when he returned home, it would be for good. It was. And if the stories they tell about Carter House are true, Captain Tod resides there still.

Tod was the middle son of Fountain Branch Carter, a prosperous merchant and farmer in the small town of Franklin, Tennessee. Tod and his brothers were loyal sons of their native soil, so when Tennessee left the Union, all three Carter boys offered their services to the Confederacy.

The eldest, Moscow, became a colonel of the Twentieth Tennessee Infantry, but by the fall of 1864, he had already been captured and paroled home. The youngest,

Frank, was wounded at Shiloh but survived. Theodoric, the middle son, had been commissioned a captain in the Quartermaster Corps.

Tod was captured during the battle for Missionary Ridge at Chattanooga and sent north. He escaped, however, and eluding Yankee patrols, made his way back to Rebel lines, where he rejoined the Army of Tennessee.

Not content with a desk job far from the front, Captain Carter soon wrangled a transfer to the staff of General Thomas Benton Smith's division. He joined the staff just in time for General Hood's Nashville Campaign of 1864.

By the autumn of '64, the war was going badly for the South. Yankee armies were everywhere, closing in on the heartland of the Confederacy. After being "Hood-winked" by William T. Sherman before Atlanta, John Bell Hood, the new commander of the Army of Tennessee, had one last card up his sleeve. Even as Sherman's lawless hordes ravaged and plundered the deep South, Hood wheeled his army about and marched north in a desperate bid to turn the tide of the war.

The Confederates had realized too late that possession of Nashville was the key to victory in the western theater. For over two years it had been the major supply depot and staging area for the northern armies, and its central location made it a strategic hub for all road and rail transportation in the west. Capture that prize, Hood reasoned, and the Federals would be hard pressed to maintain their troops in the field, while the southerners would have a windfall of munitions, livestock, and other badly needed supplies.

"On to Franklin!" Hood exhorted his new command. "Franklin is the key to Nashville, and Nashville is the key to Independence!"

The cagey commander of Union forces at Nashville, General George H. Thomas, knew Hood well. They had been at West Point together—in fact, Thomas had been Hood's instructor there, and he knew Hood was a one-trick pony, capable of only one maneuver: attacking. So, when Thomas learned of Hood's promotion, he started bringing in reinforcements from all directions.

Among the outlying commands Thomas called on was General John M. Schofield's field force in southwestern Tennessee. It quickly became a race to see who would reach Nashville first, Schofield or Hood.

A day's march south of Franklin, at Spring Hill, Hood thought he had gotten the drop on Schofield's army and had it trapped. Schofield and Hood had been classmates at West Point, and Schofield also had tutored Hood at the academy. Now, Schofield was about to give Hood a few more lessons in tactics.

It was late in the day, and Hood, thinking his prey was virtually in the bag, had gone to bed, planning to destroy the Yankee force on the morrow. But during the night, Schofield's force marched up the Columbia Pike right under the noses of the Confederates. The next morning, Hood was furious at having been outwitted again and blamed his troops for what was surely his failure—even going so far as to accuse his men of cowardice.

Schofield's orders were to get to Nashville with his command intact, but when he reached Franklin on November 30, he found all the bridges across the Harpeth River were down or seriously damaged. He therefore ordered one of his divisional commanders, General Jacob Cox, to establish a defensive position just south of town and hold Hood's army at bay until bridging equipment could be brought up. Cox's orders were clear: If he was not attacked by six o'clock that evening, he was to fall back in good order. Hold till six, then withdraw; it was a simple rearguard action.

The Carter family's house and property lay on the southern outskirts of Franklin. Their farm straddled the Columbia Pike, the very route along which the Federals were retreating. The fieldstone walls and various outbuildings of the Carter farm were spread out along a prominent crescent-shaped ridge, which offered a commanding view of the road to the south and the surrounding countryside.

In the gray light of dawn, the Carter family awoke to the sounds of soldiers trespassing through their front yard. All around them, blue-clad men were busily entrenching behind stone walls. The Union forces worked throughout the day to fortify the ridge along which the Carter farm lay—and the family's home ended up smack in the middle of the opposing battle lines.

The dwelling, known today as Carter House, was solidly built, with thick brick walls and a stout stone cellar. Colonel Carter and his father hastily prepared the basement to make it proof against gunfire and to hide their valuables from thieving Yankees. When the basement was at last secure, the colonel and his father gathered up wives, daughters, grandchildren, neighbors, and servants, and hustled them all into the safety of the spacious cellar.

Little Lena, the eldest of the Carter grandchildren, could not be found at first. She had run upstairs to fetch her prized doll-trunk. Outside, one of the boys had also tarried that afternoon; he was in the yard playing soldier—until a minié ball whizzed past, punching a hole clean through the top of his hat. The youngster made a beeline for the cellar door after that.

It was by now late afternoon, and no sooner were the Carter clan and their neighbors safely ensconced in the cellar than the noise outside increased dramatically. The battle of Franklin had begun in earnest.

It was not until well into the afternoon that Hood's main force was able to concentrate south of town, and even then, the artillery train was still well to the rear. Hood's commanders, who were better acquainted with the lay of the land than he was, advised him to bypass the Union rearguard and outflank the Yankees. It was, in any case, far too late in the day to launch an attack.

No one ever doubted General Hood's personal courage, but his judgment in the field was another matter entirely. Even Robert E. Lee, upon hearing of Hood's appointment to command the Army of Tennessee, expressed reservations. Hood, he said, was "all lion and no fox."

In the previous year alone, Hood had been seriously wounded in battle twice, each wound sufficient to qualify him for discharge. He had lost an arm at Gettysburg, a leg at Chickamauga—and some say he lost his mind at Franklin.

Disregarding all advice, Hood ordered a frontal assault on the Union defenses south of Franklin late in the afternoon. Lacking artillery support, his troops would be forced to advance across two miles of open fields in failing light against an enemy that had spent all day preparing for them. When his subordinates protested the order, Hood accused them all of cowardice.

So, for the sake of honor, the Confederate commanders carried out the general's order, though they knew it was ill-conceived. Many—like General Patrick Cleburne—put themselves at the head of their formations, for they could not in good conscience order their men to certain death if they were not willing to share that fate with them.

With the sun's last fading rays, the southerners advanced, rank upon rank, in orderly lines over the broad, wide-open fields. Fierce assaults were mounted against the Union left and right flanks, but it was in the center, where the Columbia Pike pierced the entrenchments, that the Rebels made their most determined attacks.

Regiment after regiment was thrown against the Union center and faced withering volleys all the way. Incredibly, the Federal lines began to thin and crumble under the determined assaults. In the Yankee trenches, the dead were piled eight deep, and men died standing up, for there was no room left to fall. Along the line of the Confederate advance, shattered bodies were strewn even more thickly.

All around Carter House the tide of battle swirled like a maelstrom. Several times, as the Rebels seemed on the verge of breaking through, they were forced back by fierce Union counterattacks. On into the dark, the terrible fighting swept over and around the Carter farm. From his perch in the loft of the brick smokehouse next to the house, one Union sharpshooter counted no fewer than seventeen separate Rebel attacks on that position. As one Rebel commander put it, "Hell itself had exploded in our faces."

By 9 P.M., the battle had dwindled down to an occasional flurry of musket fire, and by 11 P.M., it was quiet enough for General Cox to begin withdrawing his troops. By 1 A.M., all of the Federal troops had crossed the Harpeth and were well on their way to Nashville.

In the early hours of the morning, with the darkness broken only by the light of burning carcasses and other debris, the Carters and their friends cautiously emerged from the shelter of the basement. Even as they did, a messenger came up to bring word that Captain Theodoric Carter lay wounded on the battlefield. Moscow set off in search for his brother in the dark.

As a quartermaster, Tod easily could have sat out the battle in safety, but he chose to serve as an aide to General Smith, carrying messages to the front-line commanders, observing their progress, and reporting his observations to the divisional commander. Captain Carter observed the bloody attack literally from the front line and, at the height of the battle, led men of General William Bate's division in a desperate charge against the Union center.

Out in front of the troops, Carter sat astride his favorite steed, Rosenkrantz. With his sword held high, a black ostrich plume fluttering from his Hardee hat, Tod shouted above the din of battle, "Come with me, boys! I'm almost home!"

Leading the charge from horseback, Captain Carter made an easy target for Union sharpshooters. The whole Federal line focused on the brave young captain, and soon a wall of lead smashed into man and beast. In the space of a few minutes, Tod had received nine bullet wounds in his arms and legs, and had taken a minié ball over his right eye.

After Moscow went off to search for his sibling, the rest of the family emerged from their place of refuge. Here and there in the shadows they could see disembodied lights bobbing all over the field—lanterns held aloft by scores of family members who were searching the battlefields for the broken bodies of their loved ones.

Just before daybreak, Mary Alice, one of the Carter

grandchildren, was standing on the back porch when General Smith himself rode up to the house. The general saluted the little girl and asked, "Sissie, is this where Squire Carter lives?"

When Mary Alice answered yes, the general had her fetch her grandfather and then led Tod's father and sisters to the place where Tod had fallen. Tod Carter was still alive, but the once handsome young man's uniform was splotched all over with crimson stains. Soldiers carried his broken body on a makeshift litter the short distance to the house. Tod Carter was home for good.

After lingering on the verge of death for a few days, half delirious most of the time, Captain Carter died at home on December 2, 1864. The family obtained the last casket in Franklin in which to bury Tod, and he was interred in a nearby cemetery.

Tod Carter had lived heroically and died tragically, and now he was gone forever—or was he?

Over the years, many of the people who have visited and worked at Carter House have had experiences which they believe are proof that Tod continues to linger in Carter House—and he is not the only apparition known to inhabit the dwelling.

Since 1953, Carter House has been open to the public as a historic site, operated by local preservationists. Volunteers and professionals work together to preserve and interpret the site. One thing that makes working at Carter House different from working at the average museum is that employees often have to adjust to the home's "peculiarities."

A few years back, as a new worker was opening up the house one morning for visitors, she heard heavy footsteps overhead. It sounded like someone in a pair of heavy boots tromping about on the second floor. Thinking that some intruder had broken in to rob the collection, she rushed upstairs. Arriving on the second floor all in a huff, she found . . . no one. A thorough, room-by-room search revealed nothing that could have caused such a loud noise.

On another occasion, as an employee was passing by

the room in the rear ell where Tod had died, he saw a young man in a ragged Rebel uniform sitting on the edge of the bed. More recently, a visitor on a guided tour claimed to have seen the same figure lying in bed. The man was bloody all over and swathed in bandages to cover multiple wounds. On various occasions, visitors have heard someone pacing the floor in riding boots, and still others claim to have witnessed Captain Carter reliving the last moments of life.

Many of the staff—volunteers and professionals alike—are convinced that young Tod's ghost lingers still in the old house.

Captain Carter's tragic death and dramatic afterlife in the house naturally command one's attention, but the young captain is by no means the only spectral resident of Carter House. Many people claim to have seen an apparition in the form of a young girl. The spirit, though dead, somehow seems to be full of life, according to witness accounts.

Docent Mary West saw a ghost in the form of a small child running through the home's upstairs hall and down the staircase. Another guide, Cindy Gentry, walked into the front parlor once and felt a tug on her jacket—as if a child were trying to get her attention—but when she turned, no one was there.

In 1985, an apparition snuck up on a craftsman, Nancy Bond, who was hard at work restoring the faux masonry design in the main foyer of the house. The child ghost untied the smock of the worker's apron, then ran away giggling.

This mischievous imp is thought by some to be the ghost of Annie Vick Carter, one of Tod's sisters who had hid in the cellar during the fatal battle. Critics of this theory, however, point to the fact that all of Fountain Carter's daughters were adults at the time of the battle.

It may be that Annie's restless shade chose to return to the house of her childhood in the form of a child—choosing to remember the carefree halcyon days of youth rather than the tragedy of the Civil War and Reconstruction. There were, however, a number of grandchildren who lived at Carter House during those years, and five of Fount Carter's own children died during childhood, well before the war. Whoever the girlish apparition may be, she and Tod do not roam the home alone.

A third ghost, also thought to be a member of the Carter family, has been reported at Carter House. Taking the form of a grown woman, this apparition is a less dramatic presence and has only been sighted on rare occasions. She appeared to one staff member on at least three different occasions, calling the woman's name and then disappearing. Other workers have likewise heard their names whispered at them—as if someone were trying to reach out across eternity to communicate with them.

This last ghost is believed to be the shade of Mary Atkinson Carter, Fount's wife, who died in 1852. Hers is a gentle and welcoming spirit, say those who have encountered her. Mary is more often felt as an abiding presence than a visible entity.

Perhaps mother Carter remains in the house because two of her children still do. Some believe that so long as they still abide there, Mary will not abandon them to the dark but will continue to watch over and protect them.

All who work at Carter House, and many who visit, are sympathetic to the plight of the house and the family that once lived there, but some, it seems, are more in tune with whatever abides there than others. When I visited the house, my guide, Theresa, could vouch for no supernatural experience within the dwelling, although she was aware that others had. And, in truth, I did not see or hear anything out of the ordinary, either.

But the pain and suffering of the thousands who died there lingers on-not so much as something tangible but rather as a pervasive presence. It can be felt throughout the grounds of the antebellum home. There is little doubt its origin can be traced to that fateful day in November 1864, the day when a "terrible beauty" was born at Carter House.

13

A FAMOUS VICTORY

They say it was a shocking sight
After the field was won;
For many thousand bodies here
Lay rotting in the sun:
But things like that, you know, must be
After a famous victory.
                                            —Robert Southey

IN THE SOUTH, THE PAST IS NEVER QUITE past. It continues to dwell alongside the present—intangible perhaps, but there nonetheless. Sometimes, however, the two worlds meet, however briefly. Such is the case, it seems, with Carnton Mansion.

Carnton Mansion stands on the outskirts of Franklin, perched to the southeast of the picturesque town square, beyond the railway. Built on a grand scale, it fits the popular image of the way antebellum southern homes ought to look. Like Carter House, Carnton was caught up in the deadly events of the battle of Franklin, and, of course, it too is haunted.

In its heyday, Carnton was the center of a thousand-acre plantation. Built in 1830 by Randall McGavock, a mayor of Nashville at one point, it was one of several large estates owned by the wealthy McGavock family. During the Civil War, Carnton was the home of Randall's son, John McGavock, and John's wife, Carrie.

When war came, John became a colonel in the Confederacy.

Carnton escaped the carnage of the battle of Franklin, since it was located well away from the battlefield, but it could not escape the consequences of the bloody engagement. Throughout the afternoon and evening of November 30, 1864, and continuing for days afterward, the McGavocks threw open the doors of their home to the deluge of casualties. By the thousands, the maimed, the mutilated, the dead, and the dying came to Carnton, an unending flood of suffering humanity, washed ashore by the tide of battle.

Room after room of Colonel McGavock's spacious home filled with casualties, and still more came. Blood streaming from gaping wounds saturated Carrie McGavock's fine imported carpets and oozed through the saturated broadlooms to soak into the hardwood floors, staining them forever a deep maroon.

Soon the casualties spread out onto the lawn beyond the verandah. The living were propped up against trees, if possible, and many had to be laid out in the open till they could be treated. The dead also were laid out in the yard by the hundreds. There were so many corpses, in fact, that they had to be stacked like cordwood for lack of room. Had they indeed been firewood, there would have been a sufficient supply to warm the large and drafty mansion for many winters.

On the many-columned porch, the bodies of four Confederate generals were laid side by side, while a fifth general lay grievously wounded upstairs in a canopied four-poster bed.

Regimental surgeons and civilian volunteers toiled ceaselessly at Carnton to tend the wounded but were overwhelmed by the sheer numbers of casualties. Scores of men died of their wounds before they received treatment. In only four short hours on November 30, more than fifteen hundred Confederate soldiers died outright, while thousands more either were maimed or died of their wounds in the weeks that followed.

No one could question the bravery of the men of the

Army of Tennessee that day—except their commander, John Bell Hood, who blamed them for his failure to destroy Schofield's Federals. The Rebels hurled themselves at the Yankees with courage that bordered on the fanatical. One Confederate drummer boy—a mere child—tried to jam his drum in the mouth of a Federal cannon to disable it; it went off just as he did so and as one eyewitness put it, the boy "exploded like a tomato."

The southerners had charged into the valley of death and lost nearly a third of their army; fifty-four regimental commanders were either killed or wounded—all to take a position the Yankees would have vacated in a few hours.

Many of the slain were buried where they fell, placed hurriedly in shallow graves, with only a crude wooden marker to identify their remains. As winter closed in, temperatures plunged and the markers were taken by blacks in need of firewood. Worse still, hounds and wild beasts were also abroad that winter and scavenged many of the shallow graves for meat.

At Carnton, the mistress of the house, Carrie McGavock, put her skills as domestic manager to good use in the unpleasant task of burying the dead. As the corpses mounted like so many bales of cotton, she kept meticulous records, making sure that each soldier was identified by name and unit. On their own initiative, the McGavocks set aside acreage for use as a burial ground.

The concentration of so much anguish, pain, and death in such a relatively small area could not have failed to leave its mark on Carnton. Not surprisingly, more than one phantom in gray has been sighted on the grounds of Carnton mansion.

Perhaps the most widely reported apparition at Carnton is Cleburne's Ghost, sometimes referred to simply as "the General." This spirit appears to have been a military officer in life, and while "the Stonewall of the West," General Patrick Cleburne, is a likely candidate, he is not the only one. What most observers can agree on is that the specter haunts the halls of Carnton still.

One of the big events of modern-day Franklin's social season is the Heritage Ball, a gala fundraiser for Carnton. One year during the fête, a security guard was posted to keep watch on the party tent that had been erected on the back lawn the evening before the party. As the man was standing watch, his guard dog became very agitated, barking and yapping at someone—or something—in the shadows. The animal charged into the darkness, and despite the guard's repeated efforts to get the canine to heel, it would not heed him.

At first he thought the dog had picked up the scent of a raccoon or possum and had treed the varmint. But when the guard rounded the opposite side of the tent, his flashlight revealed a figure dressed in a long gray coat standing on the nearby verandah. The visitor seemed to the security officer to be an older man, but when he called out to him—the gray-clad figure vanished into thin air!

On another occasion, a local businessman—a prominent supporter of the museum—was coming up the driveway late one evening. As his car approached the mansion, he spotted someone sitting on the back porch, leaning his head over the railing. As the car drew closer, the man on the porch stood up and began walking away.

The businessman recalled that the face of the figure on the porch seemed blank, but the fellow was clearly dressed in a long coat and broad-brimmed felt hat—such as a Confederate officer might have worn. The apparition walked across the porch and disappeared into the shadows.

Members of the Carnton staff have had their encounters with the General as well. In fact, the staff had to remove the key from the door that leads from the upstairs hallway onto the rear verandah because the portal not only kept closing on its own but it also locked itself as well—or rather, the General kept locking it.

The General's pacing to and fro on the second-floor verandah, and his peering into the yard where the dead and wounded once lay heaped by the thousands, has led to the conclusion that the apparition is one of the officers who died there. The fact that his favorite habitat on the second floor is directly above the spot where the four Confederate generals were laid out after the battle has led some to speculate that the entity may be one of that quartet.

Others, however, theorize that the figure on the upper porch is really the ghost of Colonel John McGavock himself, the master of Carnton—who still resides there, and who is still appalled at the carnage he witnessed.

More mysterious than the General is the Weeping Maiden. This phantom inhabits the second story of the house and is most often seen in the upstairs bedroom that served as an operating room for wounded soldiers during the battle.

Described as a young woman with long, dark hair and a long, flowing dress, the Weeping Maiden is most often seen gazing out the bedroom window overlooking the front lawn. Many who have encountered this ghost report hearing a gentle sobbing sound when she is present.

At times, the Weeping Maiden has also been spotted walking across the bedroom, passing between a vintage four-poster and an antique dress mannequin, and gliding into the next room. One time, a laborer was at work in the room when he noticed the aroma of a woman's perfume. It caught his attention because there was no one else around and the fragrance was unlike anything he had ever smelled before. The man looked up from his work just in time to see the phantom female pass from the room. At other times, a stream of cold air can be felt along the route the Weeping Maiden normally follows between rooms.

The entity's close association with that particular room—the one used as an operating theater—has led to speculation that she was a civilian volunteer who served as nurse in the aftermath of the battle. Her distraught spirit remains there, disturbed by all the suffering she saw in that room.

Others theorize that the Weeping Maiden may have been the wife or sweetheart of one of the soldiers who died on the operating table. Still others discount her association with the battle at all, believing that she is from another era entirely—most likely a spurned lover or young widow whose fate was somehow linked to the house. Whatever her identity, the Weeping Maiden seems to be locked into one moment of poignant sadness for all eternity.

Then there is the noisy Kitchen Ghost. This specter, which neither weeps nor paces, and certainly is not pale or gray, is most often encountered on the ground level of the house in what used to be the kitchen area of Carnton.

Observers report objects moving around on their own in the kitchen. Staff and visitors alike have heard this agitated entity rattle pots, pans, and crockery, and when it is particularly cantankerous, it is said to actually break dishes. On one occasion, it even smashed a prized antique lamp.

In contrast to Carnton's other phantoms, the Kitchen Ghost is not associated with the War Between the States. Rather, it is believed that it is the ghost of a mulatto cook who was savagely murdered by one of the plantation's black field hands in the late 1830s. Tradition holds that the woman had spurned the man's advances and that he, having lost his head in the throes of love for her, returned the favor with a vengeance. Her severed head has been reported floating about the grounds of Carnton from time to time, still in search of its body.

Bernice Seiberling, the museum's assistant director, has a photo purporting to show a woman's head floating in midair in a hallway of the house, its face etched with a tragic grimace. This, she believes, is the noisy Kitchen Ghost.

Beyond Carnton's rear kitchen and verandah lies an entire garden of death where pale dragon's teeth of stone stand as reminders of the tragedy of war. So many individuals died such violent deaths here during the conflict that it is not surprising to hear that other phantoms have occasionally been sighted besides the three mentioned above.

Reports of apparitions roaming the grounds—apparitions not tied to any specific person or event—indicate that the old mansion still has many secrets to reveal.

A visit to Carnton Mansion—like a visit to nearby Carter House—is an awesome and inspiring experience, one not to be missed by those who live in or visit the Mid-South. Should you decide to visit Carnton, be sure to pay your respects to the General and the estate's other spectral residents—but whatever you do, don't anger the cook!

14

THE PHANTOM SIGNALMAN
OF CHAPEL HILL

THE WEATHER WAS WICKED THAT EVEN-
ing at Chapel Hill—a tiny whistlestop on the old
Louisville & Nashville line. The rain was so thick that a
man could scarcely see his hand before his eyes, and it
had been coming down in sheets all day, like an angry
demon on a rampage.

Now, with night coming on, the station attendant at
Chapel Hill was fretting as he stared out into the deepening dark. He had good cause to worry, for the evening
express freight was due at any time, and he was not at all
sure about the condition of the tracks up the line. All that
rain pooling by the embankment could well erode the
gravel bed on which the rails were laid.

Reluctantly, the old railroadman donned his slicker
and lit the large signal lamp. The lamp was so big and
bright that it could be seen for some distance even in this
weather. It would give him enough light to inspect the
rail bed and, if need be, to flag down the express freight.

So it was that the lone signalman for Chapel Hill left
the cramped comfort of his office in the depot and
trudged out into the raw, rainy night. It was slippery as
all get-out as he walked up the line; the sharply sloping
gravel embankment was doubly treacherous when it was
wet like this. He strained to keep a wary eye out for signs
of sagging or slippage on the rail bed—a telltale sign the

tracks were weakened. It was a thankless task but a necessary one.

As the signalman proceeded up the line, eyeballing every yard of track, it happened. Some think the man slipped on the gravel and was knocked unconscious when his head struck a rail. Others surmise that he was trying to signal the express to slow down when his lantern went out. Whatever the cause, the one thing that is known for certain is that the signalman was struck and killed by the speeding train that rainy night.

His body was discovered the next morning, and a relief party was deputized to perform the grim task of gathering up the man's remains—not that there was much left to gather. As workers combed the gory scene of the accident, they managed to collect what was left of the signalman's torso and limbs, and even recovered the shattered pieces of his lantern, but they never were able to find his head. Very strange, that was.

From the condition of the torso, the coroner said the signalman's head must have been sliced clean off by the steel wheels of the locomotive. What became of the head was anybody's guess. Perhaps a stray dog carried it off and had his own private feast, or perhaps someone in the search party kept it as a souvenir. At any rate, according to most accounts, this incident was the start of the sightings of a mysterious light that have chilled Chapel Hill's residents and visitors to the community for decades.

The accident remained the talk of the town for months and was a rich source of gossip and speculation whenever folks gathered 'round the potbellied stove at the general store. Sometime after that, though, talk began to center less on the accident and more on the things people were seeing down by the tracks.

Today, few people in Chapel Hill can recall when the sightings first began, they just know that, for as long as anyone cares to recall, their town has been host to the "ghost of the railroad tracks," as some call it. Outsiders refer to the unusual luminosity as the Chapel Hill Ghost Light, but to most residents of Chapel Hill, it is simply "the Light."

The truth of the matter is that, even among those who have seen the darned thing, no one is quite sure what it is. Ask five people around the town square, and you will likely get five different opinions on the subject. Tom, who works at one of the local gas stations, thinks the affair is just so much stuff and nonsense. "Ain't no ghost," he once told a reporter. "[It's] nothin' but a train; the light shines from the train and off the track. That's all."

Across the street, at another gas station, Mike tells a different story. It seems he went down to the tracks with some buddies one night, and it wasn't long before they saw a round, reddish light coming down the track toward them. That was enough for Mike and company. They skedaddled out of there before it got too close, which was a good thing, because the sheriff showed up just about the same time the light did.

Miss Lillian over at the local cafe says she has never seen the Light—but she is a believer nonetheless. Her son, Davy G., went out to the tracks one night in hopes of seeing it. At first, there was nothing but darkness, but Davy called out to it, and no sooner had he done so than it appeared.

Davy watched, amazed, as the Light came closer and closer. He stood motionless until the thing was so close he could feel heat radiating from it. When it got that near, Davy lit out of there as fast as his legs would go.

Another time, a man and two boys went to the tracks at night to check out the story of the Light for themselves. Half as a dare and half out of curiosity, one of the boys, Jack, had asked his uncle to go see the ghost light. Jack volunteered to stand by the rails while his uncle and a friend watched from a discreet distance away.

Jack was about to give up and write off the whole affair as just another tall tale when the Light appeared. At first, it came straight down the tracks almost as if it were a train, but it was no headlamp that Jack saw approaching—it seemed more like some luminous body or entity. As the trio stood there, entranced, the Light started to bob and weave as it drew closer. It seemed almost as if someone were holding a lamp at different heights and positions to inspect the line of track.

The Light appeared to halt—as if taking notice of the boy along the track—and then made a beeline straight for Jack. There was a thudding sound, and the youngster felt an unearthly, bone-chilling cold. Then the light emerged behind Jack and sped down the track, vanishing into the dark.

According to Jack's uncle and friend, who had witnessed the events from the road, the ghost light had actually passed right through the boy. "Awesome and strange" is how one writer later described the encounter.

Equally strange was the encounter four good ol' boys had with the Light one dark Friday night in the 1970s. Like many young men their age, these fellows were endowed with an excess of energy and a shortage of gray matter.

Driving about one night with no particular goal in mind, they took it into their heads to go to Chapel Hill and have some fun looking for the ghost light. Like so many others, they had heard tales about the apparition for years, and while none would openly admit to believing in it, they were all curious. Anyhow, it seemed good for a laugh or two.

Fortified, one suspects, by large quantities of liquid courage, the four pulled up to a certain railroad crossing just outside of town that was known to be one of three spots where the Light could be seen. Unlike most seekers of the Light, these four rocket scientists did not bother to park their car and walk to the tracks. Instead, they stopped the vehicle right on the crossing itself. They left the engine running, thinking they would not be there long, and no one ventured to get out of the car.

Their curiosity was rewarded—after a fashion. After a few minutes, the young men saw a light coming up the line. They heard no warning horn, but the light continued to move in a straight line, growing larger and larger by the minute, just like the headlamp of an oncoming train would. Suddenly, it dawned on the befuddled quartet that the light might just be an express freight barreling down on them, on its way to Chattanooga.

In a panic, the driver popped the clutch and stomped down on the accelerator—but the car did not move. He gunned the engine, but the auto still refused to move. There they were, astride the tracks, and in seconds the light would be right on top of them. They surely would not survive if a train were to hit them at full speed.

Closer and closer the light came, and the driver of the car still was frantically trying to shift the car into gear—forward, reverse, anything to get out of there. The young men heard no horn, but now there seemed no doubt that the oncoming light was actually a train. Instinctively, they crouched down inside the car and braced for the collision.

The light, looking now like a fiery eyed Cyclops, grew large and bright, filling the car's passenger compartment with an unearthly glow. The four young men closed their eyes and prayed for their lives.

It is said that God protects fools and drunkards, so these good old boys were doubly blessed. There was no crash, only a noise so loud that it shook the car, and then the light sped on down the tracks and disappeared.

Once the Light had gone, the car's transmission suddenly functioned once more, and the vehicle lurched forward. Off the tracks at last, the driver floored the accelerator and did not slow down until the four frightened men were many miles away and approaching the cool neon light of a gas station.

When they emerged from the car, the men noticed a series of deep scratches down the back of the vehicle. All agreed the marks had not been there when they left home earlier that evening. Who—or what—had put them there?

Next to the Bell Witch and the mysterious disappearance of David Lang, the Chapel Hill Ghost Light is the most noted unexplained phenomenon in Tennessee—and among the most famous in the South. Over the years, people have traveled from far and wide to

Chapel Hill in hopes of catching a glimpse of the mysterious Light.

At one point, some years back, strangers were coming to the tiny community at night and shooting at the Light, shooting at each other, and generally getting into all sorts of mischief. One Halloween, a Nashville television station not only ran a story on the Light but also gave out directions so viewers could look for the eerie luminosity themselves that evening.

Well, that really tore it. The local sheriff had already been inundated with complaints from people living near the haunted tracks about trespassers, and the TV people had just made the problem worse.

To remedy the situation, the sheriff and a local judge went down to Route 31 that same Halloween evening. At about 10 P.M., a veritable caravan of cars began arriving from up Nashville way, and as one carload of city folks after another pulled up to ask where they might see the Light, the two local officials directed them to a nearby road. After about fifty or so autos had turned up the lane, which was on private property, the sheriff closed the road and proceeded to arrest the whole lot for trespassing! That put a damper on things—for a while.

The truth is, living with a phenomenon like the Light gets to be old hat after a time. The people of Chapel Hill would probably prefer their town to be known as the place where legendary Confederate hero General Nathan Bedford Forrest is buried, rather than as a place to see spook lights.

For that matter, not everyone in Chapel Hill agrees that whatever is in their midst is a spook—or that he is looking for his head. But something strange dwells in Chapel Hill still—something that neither science nor reason can explain.

15

THE DAY IT RAINED
BLOOD AND GORE

THE SUN SHONE BRIGHTLY THAT WARM
Friday morning in Wilson County. It was early August,
and the Negro farm hands had been in the fields for several hours, tending the tobacco crop on E. M. Chandler's
farm. The tobacco had already grown to a considerable
height, and harvest was just a few weeks off.

A friend of Chandler's, a Mr. J. M. Peyton, had
stopped to visit from Lebanon, the county seat. The two
men sat in Chandler's house on Spring Creek that morning, conversing amiably on various topics of the day.

Suddenly, two of Chandler's field workers came running, out of breath and all in a panic. At first it was difficult to get a coherent story from the men, who were
gasping for air between words, but after a bit of ques-
tioning, Chandler and Peyton were able to make some
sense of what they were saying. And what they were saying was beyond belief: It was raining blood in the tobacco
fields!

In this day and age, such an incident may seem
bizarre but not impossible. An airplane colliding with a
flock of birds could conceivably slice and dice the foul
and thus create the same effect.

The main problem with that explanation is that there
could have been no planes in the vicinity of Wilson
County that day—the bloody rain on the Chandler farm

fell on August 6, 1841! The farm workers were Chandler's slaves, who had been toiling in the fields when the incident occurred.

About 11:30 that morning, as the field hands were working among the tall tobacco plants, they heard a rattling noise—like rain or hail—which they soon discovered was caused by drops of blood hitting the leaves and ground around them. Looking up, the workers saw a small red cloud passing swiftly from east to west. It had been directly overhead when the bloody rain began but had quickly disappeared from sight, leaving a crimson trail behind.

At first, Chandler and Peyton did not know what to make of what they'd heard. Perhaps the slaves were imagining things or, at the very least, exaggerating. Either way, the men had to see for themselves what the commotion was all about, and joined by another friend, D. S. Dew, that is exactly what they did.

When the three men arrived at the field about 3 P.M., they found that the field hands had not exaggerated. Scattered throughout the field at irregular intervals were drops of blood and small bits of flesh, fat, or gristle.

Chandler picked up one piece of tissue, measuring about an inch to an inch and a half long, that seemed to be half flesh and half fat. When he brought it close to his nose, it gave off a putrid odor.

Even though they had seen the odd bit of matter with their own eyes, Chandler, Peyton, and Dew were at a loss to explain it. The men summoned Dr. W. P. Sayle, a physician from nearby Lebanon, to assist them, and the physician hurried out to inspect the scene of the unusual occurrence. Trained as a man of science, Dr. Sayle approached the incident as rationally as possible, and his observations confirmed those of the other three men. "The extent of the surface over which it spread and the regular manner it exhibited leave little doubt of its having fallen like a shower of rain," he wrote.

Though Dr. Sayle's inspection of the site confirmed what had happened, the physician could not begin to explain it. He collected a few samples of the gory rainfall and sent them to the attention of Professor Gerard Troost at the University of Nashville.

Dr. Troost was widely hailed as one of the most eminent men of science of his day. The director of the university had brought Troost over from Europe to head the school's science department, and the scholar's presence on the faculty helped strengthen Nashville's claim to the mantle of "the Athens of the South." From his laboratory in the towers of the castle-like campus on Rutledge Hill looking north towards the city, Troost meticulously analyzed the material.

"The flesh," he reported, was "without doubt" animal matter. As for the blood drops, Troost was more cautious, stating that the material did not seem to be blood but appeared instead to be rain that had picked up red dust and "some gummy substance." Troost's cautiousness on this point may be understandable, given the small amount of the sample, but it is unlikely Dr. Sayle would have chosen a contaminated or dirty sample from the tobacco field to send to Troost. Nor does Troost venture to say what the "gummy substance" was, if not congealed blood.

Meanwhile, all the strange doings on Chandler's farm had not gone unnoticed by the local press. The *Lebanon Chronicle* sent a correspondent to interview both Chandler and Peyton regarding the incident and to inspect the field himself. The reporter closely examined the drops of blood on the tobacco and noted that the pattern of their splatter on the leaves definitely indicated they had fallen perpendicularly-proof they had come *vertically* from the sky and had not been sprinkled on the plants at ground level, which would have created a telltale teardrop pattern on the leaves.

The reporter also provided a reasonably accurate record of the extent of the bloody rain. By his estimate, the part of the field covered by gore measured some forty to sixty yards wide and at least six hundred to eight hundred yards long. But the reporter also noted that "a forest on the east and a field of weeds on the west prevent our tracing it beyond the green tobacco." The material was widely distributed over the field, which served to corroborate the slaves' account that the cloud—if that is indeed what it was—appeared to be moving at a very high rate of speed.

Within a few weeks, the Nashville papers picked up the story, adding to the furor surrounding the incident. From the outset, newspaper reports of the phenomenon were regarded with more than a little suspicion because the eyewitnesses were Negro slaves. It was only due to Chandler's personal affirmation of the veracity of his field hands that the white community was willing to accept their testimony.

While farmer Chandler and his friends may have been open-minded about this uncanny experience, it is unlikely that many of his neighbors would have been so inclined. Like the residents of Ambrose Bierce's fictional "Blackburg," where blood and gore rained down, many of Chandler's neighbors probably would have regarded the incident as an ill omen; they would have seen Satan, not Science, at work.

With all the public attention focused on his farm, Chandler must have found it very difficult to get the farm chores done. With the tobacco harvest rapidly approaching, such disruptions could mean financial disaster for the farmer—and this may go a long way toward explaining what happened next.

No sooner had Dr. Troost published his findings in the scholarly press than he issued an embarrassed retraction. According to press reports, Troost explained that the slaves had recanted their story, saying that the bloody rain had just been a hoax perpetrated by the slaves "for the sake of practicing upon the credulity of their masters." With this announcement, the press and nearly everyone else quickly lost interest in the affair, and things quickly returned to normal on the busy Chandler plantation.

Although a convenient explanation had been given for the weirdness in Wilson County, inconsistencies persisted. There was physical evidence—independent of the eyewitness testimony—that corroborated the accounts of blood and gore raining from the sky. Also, it is quite un-likely that a handful of Negro slaves—whose position was tenuous to begin with—would go to such elaborate lengths to embarrass the man who had the power of life and death over them. Moreover, the effort required to perpetrate such a hoax would seem to far exceed any benefit that could be derived from it.

Beyond all this, the fact remains that the bloody rain of 1841 closely parallels similar events that have oc-curred elsewhere in our space-time continuum. Those incidents were not deemed to be hoaxes—and there is considerable reason to believe that the strange rain in Wilson County was not one, either.

Charles Fort, the eccentric researcher who first in-vestigated this sort of phenomenon, noted that there is a "sociologically necessary determination to have all falls accredited to earthly origin." One cannot help but feel that something like that imperative was at work here. It was easier for all concerned to discredit the testimony of a few field hands than to accept the uncomfortable truth of what happened.

The bloody rain in Wilson County was uncanny but not unique. In fact, a few decades later and some miles north of the Chandler farm, an event of striking similar-ity visited another part of the Dark and Bloody Ground.

This incident occurred in Bath County, Kentucky, about three miles south of Olympian Springs. Again, a small farm was the site of the strange visitation, but there could be no question about the veracity of the eyewit-nesses.

Allen Crouch and his wife, Rebecca, were simple, hard-working country folk. The demands of farm life re-quired that both spouses work long hours to survive. While Allen toiled in the fields, Rebecca's days were filled with housework, cooking, tending to the livestock, and an assortment of other chores. One such task was making lye soap, and it was this chore that Rebecca was working at on Friday, March 3, 1876.

Rebecca had made lye-water from the ashes collected from her winter cooking fires and was combining them with rendered fat in her cauldron outdoors to make the traditional southern soap. It was an ordinary March day, with a clear blue sky above.

While she was busy with her task, drops of blood and small pieces of meat began falling from out of the blue. The raw flesh fluttered down all about her in small strips, most about the size of snowflakes, although a few measured three to four inches in diameter.

As had happened earlier in Wilson County, the flesh and blood fell in a linear band, in this case about one hundred fifty feet wide and at least three hundred feet long. By the time the gory rain ceased, blood and pieces of meat were scattered all over the fences, trees, and ground in the Crouch family's barnyard and two adjacent hillsides.

As it came down, the meat looked very much like beef and was evidently quite fresh. Rebecca was not the only one to witness the strange event. Two men near the scene were even bold enough to taste this unearthly manna from heaven and proclaimed that it tasted like mutton or venison.

Understandably, the incident raised considerable commotion in the quiet little community, and reporters soon were interviewing the neighbors. From the local *Bath County News,* the story was picked up by the Louisville papers, and finally by the national media. Scientists from Transylvania College in Lexington made the fifty-mile trek into the hills to investigate.

These eyewitnesses' testimony could not be discounted on racial grounds, so various rationalizations were put forward to try to explain away the strange downpour of blood and gore. One creative scholar even theorized that some flying scavenger had overeaten and then regurgitated while over the Crouch farm. This hypothesis had a serious flaw: It was estimated that the equivalent of half a wagonload of meat had fallen from the sky—considerably more than even the largest buzzard or other airborne scavenger could possibly consume.

Even more imaginative than the "vomiting buzzard"

theory was one scientist's attempt to classify the meat as nostoc, a type of algae. Despite the eyewitness accounts, this scholar argued that the matter had been there all the time and simply sprouted in the wake of a rainfall. That the substance had fallen from the sky, that it was red and not green, or that several persons had sampled it and declared it to be meat, does not seem to have disturbed this scientist in the least.

Then, as now, many academics were loath to let facts get in the way of their theories. But, assuming one is interested in the truth, what are we to make of all this? Fortean falls, as such events are known, have been documented over a wide span of time and space, and continue to occur even today. The incidents in Wilson County, Tennessee, in 1841 and Bath County, Kentucky, in 1876 are not isolated events. What makes them unique is that the material which fell from the sky was not composed of inanimate objects or small animals but finely minced meat and blood of some sort. None of the known incidents of Fortean rains have ever been adequately explained, and these are the rarest and strangest of all.

The celebrated science writer Arthur C. Clarke dubbed this phenomenon "high strangeness," and indeed it is. That rains of blood and gore should fall upon a realm known as "the Dark and Bloody Ground" is ironic at the very least—and perhaps more than mere coincidence.

At any rate, all of this makes one wonder if, perhaps, Chicken Little wasn't right after all.

16

THE HAINTED LITTLE CHURCH AT BIG SPRINGS

MIDDLE TENNESSEE HAS LONG BEEN known as "the Buckle of the Bible Belt." Churches large and small abound in a sometimes bewildering assortment of denominations throughout the region. Even the remotest community can boast at least one meetinghouse that serves as its spiritual and social center.

Religious revivals traditionally are important yearly events in the life of these godly folk. In late summer, when the crops have been harvested and the tobacco is curing in the barns, people take time out from their daily chores and go to the big tent meetings and revivals in hopes of attaining a great spiritual awakening. At the very least, they can look forward to some fiery preaching and a festive get-together with friends and neighbors.

In the little church at Big Springs one summer, however, the members of the congregation got far more than they ever bargained for.

Near as anyone cares to remember, it was a fellow named Epinetus Carlock who first settled the part of Rutherford County that is known today as Big Springs. Around 1838, Epinetus was traveling through the region, and when he stopped to water his horses, he saw the verdant hills, the fertile valley, and the everlasting spring, and decided he had found a place to make his home.

Soon, other like-minded settlers established farms in the area. When that old buffalo trail was converted into a stagecoach route connecting Nashville and Chattanooga, even more folks flocked there, and the village became known as Carlockville.

About 1846, a preacher by the name of A. J. McNabb established a Baptist church there and called it New Hope. For many years thereafter, the good folk of the valley would come on Wednesday nights and twice on Sunday to hear him preach on the torments of hell and the rewards of heaven, and in the summer the pastor would lead them in a week-long revival at the little white frame church on the hillside.

The decades came and went in the small rural community, and not much of anything happened there as far as anyone can remember. But in the late 1880s, there was a revival to end all revivals—one that is still talked about by their children's children's children.

It was late August, and as they did every year, everybody in the valley started preparing for the big meeting. The men made sure the spring was cleaned out and the horses were shod, while the women washed and ironed the family's best clothes, spruced up the house (in case of guests), and did all the necessary baking and cooking.

When the day of the revival came, people came from near and far. Those from the other side of the hill would stay with relatives or friends in the village. Those who lived closer to town but lacked a buggy or riding horse would get an early start and walk into the village, shoes in hand. Just before arriving at the revival, the women would stop to wash their feet, put on their shoes, and puff their faces with store-bought makeup.

No one could quite remember what topic the minister preached on that night, but it must have been a mighty powerful sermon. According to local lore, the rafters fairly shook as he spoke of the terrors of sin and damnation, and the more he preached of fire and brimstone, the more real they seemed to become to the congregation.

Exactly what happened next remains a matter of

some dispute, even among those who live in Big Springs today. That it happened, however, is not disputed.

The preacher reached the emotional peak of his sermon, summoning fire down from heaven, as it were. Suddenly, his words seemed to become manifest before the congregation's bewildered eyes.

Someone heard a loud noise near the pulpit, close to where the clergyman was standing. It sounded to some as if a tin plate of coins had fallen to the floor. Others said the sound was more like chains—big log chains—rattling and shaking loudly enough to raise the dead. Still others claim the noise started as a low rumbling in the attic, and then a light appeared in the attic and floated downward, stopping right in front of the pulpit.

As the light descended, it took the shape of a barrel—a barrel of chains—and then rumbled straight down the center aisle of the church. Smoke and flame seemed to erupt from both ends of the barrel as it rolled and rattled along, and pews soon began tumbling over and over. Whether the pews were tumbling about due to supernatural forces, as some people claimed, or whether they were knocked about by worshippers scrambling to get away from the mysterious barrel is a mite uncertain. What is certain is that the barrel struck abject terror into the hearts of every man, woman, and child there.

Clem Banks had been out on the steps getting a breath of fresh air that hot August night when the commotion started inside. He heard the clanking and rumbling, and had started to climb back up the wooden steps to see what all the racket was about when the barrel suddenly burst through the church doors. There it was, large as life, spewing forth smoke and flame as it rattled down the steps straight at him!

Needless to say, Clem quickly jumped out of the barrel's path and watched as it rolled down the steps. Right behind the barrel came most of the people who had been inside—at least those who could run, walk, or crawl.

But the fiery barrel had not quite finished with the folks at New Hope Church. It rolled over and over around the churchyard, spooking the horses and mules. All the animals broke loose and ran for the hills as fast as their hooves could carry them—all except for one very stubborn old mule that refused to budge, even for the thrashing barrel.

Some of the men took refuge from the terrible visitation by hiding in the crawlspace under the church, peering out between the pillars that formed the church's one foundation. After what seemed an eternity—but was really a few brief minutes—the fiery barrel rolled and clanked its way down the hill and disappeared into a patch of woods.

Dazed and bewildered, the frightened worshippers emerged from their hiding places, dusted themselves off, and then proceeded to walk home. Their animals had been so spooked that they had run all the way back to their respective barns, where they were later found, wet and shivering and half scared to death—much like their owners.

In the weeks that followed, the incident was the source of much speculation. That it was supernatural in origin was not doubted, but what did it mean?

The eerie event was generally interpreted as an indication that some great sin had been committed by a member of the congregation. The story went around that a traveling peddler—what they called a pack peddler in those days—had taken lodging for one night with a church member. Discovering that the visitor had a large sum of money on him, the man murdered the pack peddler and hid his body. Later, overcome with guilt, the man donated the money to help build the church. The building was therefore tainted with blood money—and no good could ever come of it.

The visitation by the mysterious barrel was far from the end of the affair. It was actually the beginning of a whole series of strange and uncanny events that centered on the little church at Big Springs. To most in the community, the neighborhood in which the church was located became the abode of boogers and haints—malignant spirits and ghostly presences—especially in the dark of the night.

The night following the barrel's dramatic appearance, a number of folks claimed to have heard the sound of rattling chains coming from the church, while other passers-by reported hearing benches tumbling over and over inside—even when the building was locked up tight for the night.

Not long after the barrel incident, Aunt Dolly, another member of the congregation, saw weird lights coming at her from the other side of the creek, near the church. And she wasn't the only one to see the mysterious lights; Quint Summers reported that an egg-shaped light had followed his buggy along that same stretch of road.

After another Wednesday night service, as members of the congregation were heading home in their wagons, many attested that the stars began to fall "all over them." This was apparently more than just a simple case of shooting stars in the evening sky, as the "stars"—whatever they were—came cascading down to the ground all around, scaring churchgoers and their horses half to death.

The mysterious events at Big Springs went beyond weird lights. Apparitions began to make themselves visible to passers-by, and a general dread of the church and its graveyard hung over the community. Several people even had an encounter with a headless ghost.

Ed Prater was riding home one night, and it so happened that his route took him past New Hope. A headless ghost—he thought it may have been female—jumped onto the back of his horse and rode part of the way home with him. Ed was so badly spooked by the experience that, as soon as he came within sight of his home, he jumped off his mount and ran into the house, leaving the still-saddled steed to run loose.

Other folks told of hearing a baby crying when they passed in front of the church one night. It was said that if one walked over to a certain tombstone and touched it—much like a parent touches the side of an infant's cradle—the crying would suddenly stop.

Not everyone, of course, encountered these apparitions. It was widely known that some folks were more susceptible to being haunted than others. There was old Billy Brown, for example. Billy was a preacher, and thus a godly man, but he was so sensitive to the spirit world that he would not go anywhere unless he was accompanied by his grandchildren. Billy believed that if he went out by himself, he would "see everything" and would be certain to run afoul of some malevolent entity, and that was an experience he could do without. As Granny Todd put it, "Some folks can see haints; some can't."

For some fifty years the little church on the hillside at Big Springs had been the social and spiritual heart of the small rural community. But the wood frame building had seen better days, and its supernatural reputation had taken a toll on the congregation. So, in 1901, the old church was torn down, and a new building was erected across the road on a piece of level ground.

Once the final nail was driven into the last board of the new church, the good folk at Big Springs were pleased to find that all the supernatural strangeness had gone. There was peace in the valley once more.

It has been nearly a hundred years now since those unusual events took place at Big Springs, but there are still many in the area who will not pass that way after dark. As one old-timer told a researcher who investigated the phenomenon some years back, "I don't believe in boogers, but I ain't sayin' I wouldn't run!"

17

HELL'S HALF ACRE:
SPECTERS OF
STONES RIVER BATTLEFIELD

OVER THE YEARS, STRANGE AND INEX-
plicable incidents have happened along the Stones River.
Phantom soldiers and haunted woods are but a few of the
unusual occurrences on the ground where men in blue
fought those in gray.

On a dreary December day in 1862, General William
S. Rosecrans—Old Rosey to his men—led forty-seven
thousand Federal troops out of the comfort of occupied
Nashville. Awaiting him at Stones River was Braxton
Bragg's bold Army of Tennessee, some thirty-eight thou-
sand men strong.

Rosecrans thought his destiny lay on the road to the
south—he believed he would be the hero to shatter the
Confederacy. Rosecrans's trusted chief of staff, Lieu-
tenant Colonel Julius Garesche, was also a man of destiny. But Garesche's destiny was of a far different sort
than was his commander's—for down that southerly
road, Garesche would have a rendezvous with death.

Many soldiers during wartime have a presentiment
of their own death. With friends and comrades dying all
around, it's not hard for a man to believe that he will be
next. But Julius Peter Garesche's feeling of doom had
nothing to do with close scrapes on a battlefield. His pre-

monitions of a violent death had begun many years before—in fact, Garesche knew the day of his death more
than a year before it actually occurred.

Garesche and Rosecrans were old comrades. They
had attended West Point together, Garesche graduating a
year ahead, with the class of 1841. It was at West Point
they became friends and their destinies became inter-
twined.

Soon after graduating, Julius saw the first omens of
his death. Before taking up his first posting, he had gone
back to Missouri to help his father take possession of
some land. While sleeping in a line cabin one night with
family and associates, he and the others were nearly
drowned when the riverbank gave way, tumbling the
cabin into the river just seconds after Garesche had made
his escape.

When recounting the incident to his brother, Frederick, the latter became convinced that there was something more than mere luck involved in Julius's survival.
The Garesches were Catholics—devout Catholics—and
none was more devout than Fred. Fred saw in the incident a portent—an omen that Julius would meet an untimely and violent death.

Julius took the prophecy by his mystic brother to
heart and in the ensuing years interpreted each brush
with danger or piece of ill fortune as another omen of his
impending doom. At the outbreak of the war, when several pro-Rebel relatives condemned him for siding with
the Union, the pious Major Garesche swore at them, taking the Lord's name in vain. This act, he believed, had
sealed his doom.

When he consulted his brother for advice, Frederick,
now a priest, confirmed his worst fears. In a moment of
crystal clarity, Father Fred had the veil of time lifted from
his eyes and predicted that, within eighteen months,
Colonel Garesche would meet a violent and bloody
end—dying in his very first battle.

At first glance, fate would seem to have been favor-
ing Julius, for as a staff officer in Washington, there was
precious little chance of him being exposed to enemy

gunfire. But when his old friend William Rosecrans was made commander of the Army of the Cumberland, Old Rosey tapped Garesche as his chief of staff.

So it was that the end of December 1862 saw Julius Garesche riding beside his old friend and commander in the vanguard of an army, heading toward his first engagement with the enemy—and his rendezvous with destiny.

By the evening of December 30, Rosecrans's army was deployed along the north bank of Stones River, facing Bragg's equally determined troops arrayed on the south bank. Before turning in for the night, Rosecrans gave orders to attack at 7 A.M.; his opposite number, General Bragg, ordered his commanders to attack at first light. The fate of the next day's battle would hinge on that small difference in orders.

Dawn's early light saw the massed divisions of Bragg's Confederate army slam into the right wing of an unprepared Federal army. Many of the Yankee units were still eating breakfast, their weapons stacked. The Rebels were among them before they knew what was happening.

General Richard Johnson's division was the first to feel the blow and collapsed like an eggshell. Next in line, General Jefferson C. Davis's division managed to make a scrap of it, but it was overwhelmed and had to make a fighting withdrawal through the woods. Davis's stand, however, did buy enough time to allow George Thomas's and Philip Sheridan's troops to prepare for the Rebel riptide coming their way.

The feisty little Sheridan set up his division's skirmish line in an open field without any cover. His command repulsed three successive Confederate assaults before he, too, was forced to give ground.

The sounds of battle from beyond the cedars gave Rosecrans and Garesche the first clue that something was amiss. Soon, men in blue were streaming back out of the woods toward the Nashville Pike, where Rosecrans's headquarters lay.

The devout Garesche had attended mass that morning and received the sacraments in preparation for the upcoming battle. Now, as the battle began to warm up, he and Rosecrans rode up and down the line of battle to steady their men and form a new line. Someone saw Garesche briefly dismount and go to a small clump of trees behind the pike and open his prayer book—as if he were making his last peace with God—then remount and catch up with Rosecrans.

By now the Rebels were pressing Old Rosey's troops on two sides—from the west and the south—and the general and his staff were desperately trying to cobble together an effective line to make their last stand. Mounted on their steeds, he and Garesche were prime targets for southern sharpshooters and artillery.

Suddenly, a loud report was heard from the enemy lines, and a shell came crashing through the cedars, barreling straight at Rosecrans and his staff. The munition exploded near the officers, and in a flash, Julius Garesche's head was vaporized.

Shrapnel from the same shell tore off Sergeant Richmond's thigh and had enough force left to drill a hole through the neck of an orderly's mount. Garesche had taken the shell meant for Rosecrans.

Garesche's horse trotted away, bearing its headless rider still erect in the saddle. After riding some distance down the line, the beheaded body keeled over and slumped to the ground.

It had been fifteen months since Father Fred had predicted his brother's demise, and true to the prophecy, Julius Garesche had kept his rendezvous with death.

Rosecrans had no time to mourn his friend. With Garesche's gore still splattered all over his uniform, Old Rosey rode up and down the line exhorting his men to fight.

Meanwhile, the Rebel onslaught had begun to run out of steam in the thickets and groves of the cedar forest to the west of the pike. Without orders or direction, pockets of Union soldiers began to resist; in one place, limestone outcroppings served as natural rifle pits. The same sharp rocks broke the axles of the Rebel artillery and so the southern infantry had to advance without support, fighting hand to hand in the murky, smoke-filled forest.

They called this part of the battlefield, "the Slaughter Pen," as apt a name as any for the carnage that went on there. Another spot of the field was called "Hell's Half Acre"—but that day the devil ran roughshod over considerably more than half an acre.

When the Confederate infantry at last broke through the northern tip of the woods, they thought they had the Yankee army surrounded—just make it up the rise and they would be at the pike.

But as the Rebels charged over the open field and up the slope, the guns of the Chicago Board of Trade battery opened fire. Canister, ball, and shrapnel rained down, ripping flesh and maiming. Within minutes, all that remained of the brave Confederate brigades were tattered banners and a cornfield full of mangled corpses. They too, had met their rendezvous with death.

"Wild enough for a banquet of ghouls" is how one Rebel colonel described the scene in the Cedar Glade that night. All about the survivors, the dead lay frozen in contorted positions, and the living felt somehow unwelcome in that glade of death. It was not simply a case of battlefield jitters. From that day until the present, many people have reported strange occurrences in that fatal forest— and on the battlefield in general.

Today, a large part of the Stones River Battlefield is preserved as a national park. Open to the public only during daylight hours, it offers a small museum, hiking trails, and nine interpretive stops that help explain the course of the bloody battle to visitors.

On a bright, sunny summer day, the verdant splendor of Stones River National Military Park stands in stark contrast to the suffering that once took place there on two dark days in December. Near the museum and ranger station, the hypnotic sounds of warbling birds and humming insects in the open fields can almost lull one into a sort of dream state.

But down the road a piece, at Stop Number Two,

things are different. Here, in the heart of the Cedar Glade, the shadows rule. Even on the hot and humid August day we visited, a deathly cold pervaded the Glade—an unnatural cold, magnified tenfold by the eerie silence that pervades the woods. No bird's song or bee's hum lightens the gloom of that glade. It is this very spot that Confederate Colonel William Preston thought fit for a "banquet of ghouls."

My family and I had driven out from Nashville to Stones River Battlefield on a day trip. After visiting the Interpretive Center (Stop Number One), we halted at Stop Number Two to explore a bit more.

Here and there among the towering cedars jut low limestone shelves, jagged gray things that are wicked-looking and sharp. The footpath winds in and out along the rocks and goes deeper into the forest to show visitors points of interest relating to the battle.

On entering this glade, our children, who moments before had been gay and laughing, suddenly became quieter and noticeably jittery. Neither of the older ones could put their finger on anything specific that was causing their uneasiness, but it was definitely a strong sensation—akin to the feeling one gets when walking through a graveyard late at night.

Adults have been conditioned by society to treat such feelings as foolish superstition—but younger children have not yet been so brainwashed and are more in tune with their natural instincts. My two school-age children were old enough to be aware of that sensation, yet not so old to have suppressed it.

In truth, even my wife and I had an inkling of something eerie about the place—as though someone unseen were watching us. At any rate, after a few minutes, my wife and I walked on ahead, while the kids inspected a ruined artillery piece.

Not far up the trail, but out of sight of the Slaughter Pen, I became aware of a considerably lighter feeling—as if a weight had been lifted off me. At the same time, it seemed definitely warmer, and there were birds in the trees in this part of the woods.

Suddenly, my two grade-schoolers came running up the path as if the devil himself were chasing them. They had turned around and discovered that my wife and I were gone, and finding themselves alone in that dread glade, they had been overcome by the spirit of the place and fled in terror. For the rest of the visit, they stayed close by us, fearing that whatever invisible entity had stalked them might come back.

While it would be easy enough to dismiss such experiences—the bitter chill on a hot summer day, the overwhelming sense of dread, the area of utter silence in an otherwise lively forest—were it not for the fact that other visitors have had similar experiences.

A psychic, Dale Kaczmarek, visited Stones River Battlefield some years ago. At Stop Number Four, he encountered sensations similar to those we had experienced at Stop Two. He later said he had felt "very paranoid, like I wasn't alone," and also had the sensation of being stalked by something unseen.

Dale also noticed a significant drop in temperature at Stop Four. Such "cold spots" are generally interpreted by students of the paranormal as focal points of supernatural phenomena, or "hauntings."

From time to time, visitors to the Cedar Glade have complained that someone—or something—was following them. Park rangers investigating such reports generally find no living being at the spot.

By all accounts, even the rangers have had strange encounters on the battlefield. The park closes at 5 P.M. daily—no visitors are allowed after the sun sets and no camping is allowed—so most people do not actually get to see the ghosts that dwell in Hell's Half Acre and other sites. The rangers are not so lucky.

One night, a ranger was standing guard over some property that belonged to a local reenactor group. Returning to the administration building for water, the officer noticed someone in the undergrowth as he passed by Stop Six.

At first, the ranger thought the person might be another officer who was patrolling the field. But when the man did not respond, and instead started toward him in a threatening manner, the uniformed ranger ordered him to halt and drew his revolver. The shadowy figure fell to the ground and disappeared. The ranger searched the area but found no sign that anyone had been there. Was the shadowy figure the shade of some soldier who had been killed there?

That ranger, at least, was convinced that he had encountered the ghost of a Civil War soldier who was reliving the moment of his death. At other times, reenactors encamped on the battlefield have claimed that they are sometimes joined around their campfires at night by similarly clad visitors who are not part of their group—and perhaps not of this earth.

Ambrose Bierce, who fought at Stones River with Rosecrans, told a number of strange tales relating to the battle, each as eerie in its own way as the circumstances surrounding Julius Garesche's death. More recently, there have been occasional reports of a headless horsemen riding up and down the old Nashville Pike—but whether it is the good colonel looking for his head or not, I cannot say.

A death foretold and a victory forestalled—and the devil to pay all along the way. As is the case elsewhere in the realm of the Dark and Bloody Ground, the long shadows of the past reach out to touch us at Stones River.

If the testimony of those who have walked and worked there is to be believed, there are far more than just shadows lurking beneath the brooding cedars of Stones River Battlefield.

18

REAP THE WHIRLWIND

IT WAS UNCOMMONLY HOT THAT WED-
nesday—even for summertime in the Cumberland Basin.
Ed Sharp had been working at farm chores all morning
long, and by noon it was getting too hot to bear much
more. A storm—any storm—he thought, would help
break the ungodly heat.

It was getting close to dinnertime—in the country,
folks eat their main meal in the early afternoon and have
a light supper towards dark—but Ed never got a chance
to come in out the heat for a bite to eat.

Ed's farm was only five miles out of Ashland City—
just a good stretch of the legs. But it was Merchant's Day,
and most stores would be closed, so it was no good
dreaming up an excuse to go into town, even though that
would have been a welcome relief from the hot farm-
work. But things would soon get a lot hotter for Ed Sharp.

Despite the torrid weather, Ed's wheat crop had
needed to be cut and bundled in sheaves. Using the hay
cradle was backbreaking, and it took a strong arm and
good coordination to use it without wasting a lot of time.
But he'd managed to get all the wheat cradled at last.

As Ed was busily at work—or as busy as the heat
would allow—he got that storm he'd been praying for.
But as they say, be careful what you pray for because you
just may get it!

From out of the north it came. It was not your ordinary gully-washer by any means. No dark clouds gath-

ered on the horizon, and no cool rain fell from heaven that day. What Ed Sharp got instead was a whirlwind.

It came along over the nearby woods toward his fields, not a particularly unusual incident on a hot summer day. But as it got closer, Ed and some of his neighbors noticed something very peculiar. The whirlwind was moving at about five miles an hour, and it was doing something no other tornado or wind had ever done before: It was setting fire to everything in its path!

As it moved through the forest, branches and leaves were sucked into funnel's vortex and set afire. An official report later described the vortex as "a sort of flaming cylinder."

The whirlwind cut a flaming swath through the woods, but not content with this antic, it seemed to grow in strength as it approached. Passing over Ed's draft animals, it set their manes and tails on fire, scorching them down to the roots.

The firestorm next made for his farmhouse, igniting haystacks all along the way. When it reached Ed's home, the funnel blazed along the length of the house, igniting the roof shingles from one end to the other. Within ten minutes, the entire house was wrapped in flames.

The pillar of fire continued to Ed Sharp's wheat field, incinerating the stacked wheat in its path. It passed through the field and another stretch of woods, where the green leaves on the branches were "crisped to tinder" by the whirlwind as it cut a swath twenty yards wide.

All this while, the fiery cyclone was headed toward the Cumberland River, and when it emerged from the woods and struck the waterway, it changed direction, heading downstream. Raising a column of steam as it vaporized the water, the pillar of fire continued down the river for half a mile. Finally, the vast amount of water it had sucked up took its toll on the mysterious whirlwind of fire, and it dispersed.

By the time it was all over, some two hundred people had seen the fiery storm ravage Ed Sharp's farm. His crops burned, his woods set afire, and even his house incinerated—all in all, it was a bad day for Ed Sharp.

MUSIC CITY MYSTERIES

19

PHANTOMS OF THE OPRY

THE ORNATE RED BUILDING HAS BEEN known by many names in its time: Union Gospel Tabernacle, "Mother Church," Sam's House, the "old" Opry House—or simply the Ryman Auditorium. Whatever one calls it, this old collection of brick and stone has been synonymous with the very best in country music for generations.

Perhaps more than any other place, this century-old building has epitomized the spirit of America and its music. Celebrities from Teddy Roosevelt to Bob Hope have walked its stage; Enrico Caruso and Elvis Presley have performed there. Its very floorboards seem to ooze an aura of greatness.

Even the casual visitor cannot help but feel a certain eerie presence on entering the venerable music hall. According to many who have visited and worked at the Ryman, more than just memories haunt its hallowed halls, though: Spirits of a much stranger kind have been seen performing in this venue.

Each year, tens of thousands of visitors flock to Nashville with an almost religious fervor to visit the favorite haunts of country music stars. If these fans sometimes seem more like pilgrims to Mecca than casual vacationers, who is to say that, when they visit the Ryman and trod the same stage that Roy Acuff and Minnie Pearl performed upon, and gaze out onto the old curving rows of benches, they are not—at least on some level—tapping into some deep spiritual well-spring?

The Ryman Auditorium was first and foremost a testament to the faith and spirit of one man: Captain Tom Ryman. "Steamboat Tom" was, by all accounts, something of a hellraiser in his youth. Like many rivermen, Tom drank and cursed and fought his way up and down the Cumberland, Ohio, and Mississippi Rivers. One day, however, Captain Tom heard the words of the legendary preacher Samuel Porter Jones and was converted.

From that time on, Ryman shunned all vices. He banned liquor and gambling on his steamboats and closed his saloon on lower Broadway in Nashville. As part of his newfound faith, Captain Tom also began a campaign to build a place dedicated solely to religious revivals.

His efforts bore fruit in 1892 with the opening of the Union Gospel Tabernacle on Fifth Avenue North. Though it was only a stone's throw from the notorious Black Bottoms district, Tom Ryman envisioned it as a place where people of all faiths could join together to praise the Lord.

From the first, however, the building was used as a public hall where the issues of the day could be discussed and the latest cultural refinements viewed and appreciated. The most notable event in the facility's early days occurred in June of 1897, when a large reunion of Confederate veterans was held in Nashville.

The reunion was so large that organizers had to add a balcony to the structure to accommodate the overflow crowd. While those graying Rebels could be a rowdy bunch, they were appreciative of the hospitality the city and the auditorium extended to them, and many donated money to pay for the balcony's construction. It was named the Confederate Gallery in their honor. Seats in the Confederate Gallery were always cheaper than those closer to the stage, and the gallery crowd had a reputation for being rowdier than the rest of the audience.

One of the visitors to the gallery over the years has been a mysterious gray-clad figure who has been sighted in the balcony from time to time. He has never been observed during performances, but when the audience has gone home and the "graveyard shift" is cleaning up, the Man in Gray has been seen in the gallery, silently peering down at the stage. He sometimes has been reported sitting up there during rehearsals as well.

Whenever a security guard would be sent upstairs to evict the gatecrasher, he would find no evidence of the visitor's presence. But when the guard returned downstairs, the Man in Gray would again be seen seated in the same spot in the Confederate Gallery.

Who is this strange visitor? Could it be the shade of a Confederate veteran who enjoyed the reunion so much that his spirit keeps returning to its old haunts? Is the Man in Gray some deceased patron waiting for a stage performance that will never begin? Or is he just a figment of some workmen's imaginations, the result of working in a nearly empty building late at night? One cannot say for sure whether any of these theories is the right one—but if the Man in Gray is a ghost, he is not the only one who haunts the Ryman.

Captain Thomas G. Ryman died in 1904, and by that time the old riverman was so loved and respected that some four thousand people crowded into the Union Gospel Tabernacle to attend his funeral. The Reverend Sam Jones himself led the ceremony. It was during the funeral oration that Jones proposed that the hall be renamed the Ryman Auditorium.

Considering how closely linked Tom Ryman and the old theater were, the name change was not surprising. Nor should it be surprising that, as much as the old riverman cherished the venerable hall, there are many who believe his ghost still resides there. They say that, much as he did during his lifetime, Steamboat Tom paces up and down the corridors of the building that bears his name, from the deepest cellar to the highest rafters, to assure himself that all is in order.

In the early 1900s, a production of *Carmen* played the Ryman. Bizet's opera about a woman of low morals was thought a trifle too risqué for the Ryman Auditorium, which still had the reputation of being a place of

God. It is said that Tom Ryman's ghost was present in the old pulpit underneath the stage, ranting and raving and trying to drown out the performance above him.

Since then, many believe that every time a show is staged there that does not meet the old captain's high moral standards, he tries to disrupt the presentation with preaching, the singing of psalms, or some similar act.

During the 1960s, when the Ryman was the home of the renowned *Grand Ole Opry* radio show, it was used briefly to tape live episodes of *The Jimmy Dean Show*. A crew was brought in from New York to work on the television production.

After the show had wrapped for the night, the Yankee film crew was sitting there, relaxing and chatting with the local stagehands. The locals told the New Yorkers about Tom Ryman's ghost and how he was believed to walk the theater at the stroke of midnight.

The cynical New Yorkers scoffed at the idea but decided to stick around anyway—just to see for themselves. Hours passed, and it seemed as though their wait would be a waste of time.

Shortly after midnight, however, the sound of footsteps echoed through the empty auditorium. Looking up, the skeptical northerners could see dust seeping between the edges of the ceiling panels lining the access space beneath the rafters—with each footfall, another puff of dust would emerge.

In a New York minute, the crew fled the building, hastily tossed the production equipment into a truck, and roared back north, leaving Captain Tom to his theater. Afterward, the Nashville stage crew was roaring also—with laughter. The Big Apple television crew reported the incident to one of the New York tabloids, and it briefly made headlines there.

The Ryman Auditorium has often been regarded as being synonymous with the *Grand Ole Opry*. However, it was not until 1943 that the *Opry* took up residence at the facility, and it remained there until 1974, when it moved to the new Opry House at the Opryland entertainment complex a few miles east of town. The Ryman's almost perfect acoustics and the warm, cozy atmosphere made it an ideal location for the popular weekend radio show during those three decades.

Many are the tales the old-timers tell about those days in the theater—and more than one of those tales rings of the supernatural.

"Whispering Bill" Anderson, for example, tells of the Saturday afternoon he was rehearsing on the stage of the Ryman for an *Opry* show that night. To assist the stage crew with their sound and lighting checks, Anderson played a tune on his guitar—one of the late Hank Williams's personal favorites. Suddenly, in the middle of the song, everything went completely dead—sound, stage lights, house lights, even the emergency exit lights—leaving Whispering Bill standing onstage in a total blackout.

No evidence of mechanical failure was found, and the power outage was never explained. Anderson described the experience as "eerie," adding that he felt strongly that the blackout was somehow related to his performing the Hank Williams tune.

Could the ghost of the legendary Williams also be haunting the Ryman? Perhaps, for Bill Anderson is not the only person to encounter the shade of Hank Sr. there. In the early 1990s, after being closed to the public for years, the Ryman underwent a complete renovation and modernization to allow it to host concerts again. During the construction, one of the laborers was accidentally locked inside for the night.

Alone and surrounded by countless memories of the past, the construction worker claimed to have come face to face with the late great Hank Williams. It is not known whether the apparition serenaded him with "Lonesome Blues" that night.

The renovated Ryman reopened in 1993 and today is a highly regarded venue for all manner of live performances—from "Rock of Ages" to rock 'n' roll. But at one time, the building was almost torn down to make way for a parking lot.

Shortly after the *Grand Ole Opry* moved to its new

home at Opryland, officials at the entertainment complex, which still owned the Ryman, seemed unusually eager to tear down the old theater. Their enthusiasm to destroy the venerable venue could simply be chalked up to yet another case of corporate greed, but another explanation has been offered as motivation for their actions— the Opry Jinx.

People who work closely with the *Grand Ole Opry* are understandably reluctant to discuss the Opry Jinx. On the record, they vehemently deny that such a thing has ever existed, but off the record, many are willing to concede that there may be something to the jinx after all.

The fact is that up to 1973, more than thirty-five people closely associated with the *Opry* met with untimely— at times fiery—deaths. Among the victims were a dozen of the *Opry's* greatest stars, including Jim Reeves (killed in a plane crash in 1964), David "Stringbean" Akeman (murdered by intruders in 1973), and Patsy Cline. In particular, the death of the legendary Miss Cline, who also perished in a plane crash, was surrounded by a number of supernatural circumstances. It is said that she somehow had a premonition of her impending demise. Was she aware of some invisible agency at work that others could not detect? To this day, no one knows for sure.

Curse or coincidence? It all depends on one's viewpoint, I suppose. But the eagerness of Opryland executives to demolish the Ryman in the 1970s—even in the face of overwhelming public opposition—seems very strong circumstantial evidence that someone, at least, took the Opry Jinx seriously. Perhaps all the alleged ghostly doings in the old theater had finally gotten to the corporate executives in the back office at Opryland.

Despite such tribulations, however, the "Mother Church of Country Music," filled with memories—and spirits—fulfills much the same mission as envisioned by its founder over a century ago: to be a place for "the elevation of humanity to a higher plane."

20

OLD HICKORY HAUNTS
THE HERMITAGE

ANDREW JACKSON: CONQUEROR OF THE
Creek Nation, hero of the battle of New Orleans, Seventh
President of the United States, champion of the common
man, Protector of the Union. Jackson's name and deeds
continue to resonate—and many of the decisions Old
Hickory made still affect us to this day.

It is said that if you want to understand Jackson the
politician, read the history books, but if you want to understand Jackson the man, visit his home. Today the Hermitage, Jackson's refuge from his daily cares and the
place where his beloved Rachel always awaited him faith-
fully, is open year-round to the public and operated as a
museum. The rolling meadows, the cedar-lined drives,
and stately columns of his home all look very much the
same as they did when Old Hickory lived there.

But there was a time when it seemed the house
would be allowed to return to the elements. Outside and
in, it was a shambles: The antique furniture and other
heirlooms were divided up among Jackson's heirs, and
once stripped, the building was abandoned. At one
point, the mansion even served as home for aging Confederate veterans.

Appalled at this sad state of affairs, some civic-
minded women decided to come to the Hermitage's rescue. The Ladies Hermitage Association was formed,

obtained a charter from the state, and vowed to carry out its mandate to restore the estate to its former glory.

The association took possession of the Hermitage in July 1893. But what the organization's founding members could not have known when they took possession was that the Hermitage was already possessed by Andrew Jackson's ghost!

With the Hermitage vacant, and the building not yet suitable for viewing by the public, the Ladies Hermitage Association became concerned that vandals would inflict even more damage on the old mansion. As a result, two members of the group volunteered to camp out inside the house until a suitable caretaker could be found to keep an eye on it.

So it was that early one Saturday morning in July 1893, Mary Baxter and Mary Dorris, respectively the association's regent and secretary, rode up the guitar-shaped driveway leading to the front steps of the Hermitage. The lawn was verdant with summer's splendor, and the tall cedars that lined the driveway were lush with new growth. The sighing of the wind through the leaves and branches seemed to whisper a soft welcome to the two women, adding an aura of mystery and melancholy to the place.

The sole remaining inhabitant of the once populous plantation was Uncle Alfred, an elderly Negro who took pride in telling visitors of his days as President Jackson's valet. Deaf and nearly blind, he lived in a simple log cabin behind the main house.

Due to his advanced age and physical condition, Alfred needed more help himself than he could provide to the ladies. The two women, however, had engaged a young black girl from a farm in the nearby Hopewell community to come by and prepare some simple meals for them and to help with some of the housekeeping. But she absolutely refused to stay in the old house past sunset.

The air was hot and muggy when the two Marys dismounted their carriage and walked up the peeling, whitewashed steps into the mansion, but inside, it was as cold as the grave. The parlors and halls downstairs, bereft of furniture and shrouded in dust and cobwebs, seemed desolate.

Ascending the staircase, the women took note of the elaborate wallpaper from Jackson's day, faded and torn but still prominent, that depicted a scene from Greek mythology. As they walked along the hallway on the second floor, the upper chambers seemed eerie as each footstep echoed off the bare walls.

The maid prepared a simple meal for the ladies in the cavernous fireplace downstairs and was persuaded to remain with the women long enough to help them make a thorough inspection of the house. As the trio passed from room to room, they closed and locked all the windows and doors for the night. Then a mattress was spread on the floor in the front parlor to serve as a sleeping pallet of sorts.

The two guardians had brought with them two stiff-backed wooden chairs, which they placed on the mansion's broad front porch. As they sat in the chairs, relaxing, dusk overtook them. The cook, in a panic because she had stayed so late, scurried away from the house, fearful that she would be caught on the plantation grounds when the last rays of the sun slipped below the horizon.

Shadows lengthened around Mary Baxter and Mary Dorris, and they soon had to light a kerosene lamp, which they placed on a small table just inside the main hallway to provide relief from the darkness within. As they watched the gloom gather, a piercing cry rang out west of where they sat on the porch. A reply from the opposite direction reassured them that the shrill sound was only a screech owl calling to its mate from a hollow tree.

Nevertheless, in the deepening darkness of the cedars, the weird cry served to increase the tension they felt that first night in the empty old house. They had scoffed at the cook's superstitious fear of the house, but as night closed in tight around them, those fears no longer seemed so foolish.

The moon rose over the plantation, casting its pale,

eerie light among the trees. The two ladies chatted for some time on the porch, discussing their plans for the morrow, and then, thinking the hour was late, they decided to turn in for the night. It was actually quite a bit earlier than they were accustomed to going to bed, but the quiet of the countryside and the setting about them seemed to distort the passage of time.

By the flickering light of the kerosene lamp, the women retreated to the front parlor, where they lay down on the bedding and soon drifted off into a deep sleep.

Several hours later, the two were suddenly awakened by an awful din. Nearby, in the pantry, it sounded as if someone were taking the pots and pans and throwing them all about, and emptying the cabinets of dishes and piling them on the floor.

From the porch, there came the sound of chains clanking loudly. Above them, the women could swear that they heard the sound of a horse charging up and down the upstairs hallway—as if General Jackson himself were mounted on his warhorse and riding through the halls at the head of his army!

In an instant, the ladies came fully awake and sat up on the bedding, staring in bewilderment at each other. Mrs. Baxter, the elder of the two, bade her associate to light the kerosene lamp. No sooner had she done so than the noise came to an abrupt halt.

Neither of the women dared voice her real fears. Instead, both speculated that the sounds may have been someone attempting to break in, or were made by rats— yet they knew it sounded like neither of those things. The two left the lamp lit for the rest of the night.

The next morning, Sunday, dawned clear and sunny. As scheduled, the cook returned to fix breakfast. The two guardians did not discuss what had transpired the night before, and after the morning repast, they set about their separate tasks.

On her own, Mary Dorris conducted a thorough search of the premises to determine if a natural cause could be found for the sounds. She checked closets, gazed up chimneys, inspected the cellar, and examined every possible nook and cranny imaginable. She could find nothing to account for those infernal noises.

The day passed peacefully, and after the women had completed their tasks, they walked throughout the grounds. They sat in the garden that surrounds Rachel and Andrew Jackson's tomb and meditated on the two lovers' lives, and then they read some. Other than the cook, no one visited to break the solitude. The Hermitage was well named.

As sunset approached, the self-appointed caretakers again seated themselves on the front porch. Again the sights and sounds of twilight greeted them as they watched the night enfold the plantation grounds in its dark mantle. And, as they had done the night before, they went to bed early.

This time, however, the women did not turn out the kerosene lamp but left its flame to flicker and dance about with the shadows in the room. Both drifted off to sleep with little effort and slept for several hours without incident.

But about midnight, the loud noises once more began—dishes falling in wild abandon in the pantry, chains rattling, and the distinct sound of a warhorse prancing to and fro on the second floor. Neither Mary dared to investigate the source of the strange sounds, so the ladies had to content themselves with speculating about just what the racket might be as they remained within the confines of the front parlor.

The strange happenings continued each night for the duration of the women's stay as temporary residents of the old house. Fortunately, it was not long before a full-time custodian was hired to guard the house and its grounds, and the two ladies were relieved to turn over their duties to him.

It would be some time before either Mary Baxter or Mary Dorris would talk about the uncanny happenings inside the Hermitage that July. No natural causes were ever found for the noises, but there was some indication that someone else had had a similar experience inside the house. When the women arrived that first Saturday, they had found some graffiti on the walls—no doubt written by some vagrant using the house as shelter, or perhaps scrawled by adolescents trespassing where their elders may have feared to go. At any rate, on the wall was scribbled the word "Ichabod"—and that was all.

Based on the two ladies' experiences, the name would seem to refer to the ghostly rider they had heard charging about on his trusty steed—save that, unlike the phantom Ichabod Crane encountered, Old Hickory managed to keep his head intact while galloping about the second floor of the mansion.

To our knowledge, there have been no similar incidents reported at the Hermitage since then—but no one since has ever dared to stay there past the witching hour, either. If some brave soul were to venture into those dark halls unbeckoned, no one could say for certain what surprises the old mansion may still have in store for them. If the accounts of the two women from the Ladies Hermitage Association are to be believed, the very least one could expect is a face-to-face encounter with the galloping ghost of Old Hickory!

21

MARY

WHEN ONE THINKS OF HAUNTED PLACES in the South, perhaps the last place one would imagine as a likely hangout for spirits would be the sterile corridors of a modern hospital. The coldly analytical atmosphere of a medical center, its brightly lit hallways, and its well-populated environment all run counter to our notions of the sort of place where spirits would dwell.

Yet, in the heart of one of Nashville's most respected and modern medical facilities, Baptist Hospital, just such a phenomenon was reported. Although not widely publicized at the time, scores of healthcare professionals and patients experienced a series of unusual incidents over a period of some ten years.

During the 1970s and '80s, Nashville emerged as a national center for the medical industry, and today the city's public and private hospitals boast state-of-the-art facilities and vie to provide the finest care money can buy. But it was not always so; not so long ago, Nashville's medical resources were considerably more modest in scope.

Since the turn of the century, the Daughters of Charity had run Saint Thomas Hospital on Church Street, a short distance from downtown. During the 1920s, Protestant Hospital was built across the street. Facing one another on the boulevard, the two institutions for many years served the needs of Middle Tennessee's sick and infirm, regardless of their income or social status.

By the late 1970s, however, both hospitals needed to expand to accommodate the increasing medical requirements of a growing city. Both also faced a similar dilemma: there was no room to expand. Finally, in 1974, Saint Thomas announced that it would be moving to new facilities before the end of the year. Protestant Hospital—now rechristened Baptist Hospital—would take over the old Saint Thomas buildings and use those for its expansion.

The nuns at Saint Thomas had made meticulous preparations for the facility's relocation, and when moving day came, everything went like clockwork. The nuns took everything with them to the new hospital—everything, that is, except Mary.

Mary, at least, is what the staff of the new hospital called the presence that manifested itself there. While there had been no public reports of any strange incidents before the nuns moved to greener pastures, there is no doubt that some very odd things began to occur soon after the buildings changed hands.

One room, in particular, seemed to be the focus of some unusual happenings. During the Saint Thomas era, it had been consecrated as a chapel, and there was a niche in a wall that contained a statue of the Blessed Mother—Mary. When the nuns had been packing for the move, they offered to leave the statue in place for use by the succeeding staff and patients. But the new administration declined the offer—their hospital already had a chapel in a wing of the main building.

After the statue of Mary had been removed, however, it was noticed that a nearly perfect silhouette of the Madonna remained on the wall. It was initially a source of some curiosity, since there had been no light source strong enough in that space to cause the paint around it to fade and thus create the impression of a shadow on the wall. The chapel had been located in an interior room that did not receive direct sunlight, and since the room had usually been dimmed to promote prayer and meditation, there had been no bright artificial light to cause the shadowy effect.

The silhouette remained a minor curiosity until, as part of the renovation of the new wing, workers tried to redo the room. Laborers were brought in to clean the dingy walls and eliminate the shadow, but no matter how hard they tried, no amount of scrubbing could remove the silhouette of Mary from the hospital wall.

Next, painters were summoned to cover the discoloration with a fresh coat of paint. Despite their best efforts, when the paint had dried, the shadow of Mary returned.

The work crews next tried sanding and staining the wall to eliminate the offending shadow—all to no avail. Each time, try as they might, the image of the Virgin Mary kept coming back clearer than ever. At last, the administration gave up and left the shade of Mary alone.

Those who observed the "stain" in the old chapel—including supervisors, staff, and patients—all testified to the fact that the shadow on the wall was unmistakably that of Mary, Mother of God. The inability to eradicate her image was generally attributed to supernatural forces.

Although Mary's shadow was indeed unusual, its presence was far from the only odd occurrence in that wing of the facility. In fact, a number of incidents that deny scientific explanation were also documented there.

The ghost of PICU was also believed to be somehow related to Mary's presence. One section of the old Saint Thomas complex had been converted into a Progressive Intensive Care Unit, where patients were brought after a stay in the intensive-care ward. Many of the patients in PICU had had near-death experiences and hence were still much closer to the Other Side than other patients. Nurses on duty in the unit often reported hearing strange sounds that could not be adequately explained.

On a number of occasions, nurses on the graveyard shift in PICU have sworn they heard the sound of someone whispering and a kind of dull rattling sound, such as wooden beads would make. Those familiar with such sounds readily identified them as that of someone saying the Rosary.

Nurses new to the station would often get up and try to track down the person still in the ward after hours, but they were always unsuccessful. The sound seemed to come from everywhere—and nowhere—all at the same time.

At other times, nurses posted to the unit late at night said they could hear the sound of a man talking. The tone was soft and the words were indistinct, but the voice was clear enough that they could tell it was a male speaking. The voice would drone on with this low mumbling for quite some time. Again, nurses who would try to trace the source of the sound could never quite pinpoint it. To those familiar with Catholic ritual, it seemed reminiscent of the sound a priest makes when reciting the rite of Anointing of the Sick—last rites—over a dead or dying patient.

The mumbling, whispering, and other unusual sounds encountered in PICU were usually referred to by the staff as The Bishop. It was widely believed that the sounds were uttered by some long-deceased cleric who was still making his rounds in the hospital, saying prayers over the sick and dying.

At other times, a number of staff members working in the old Saint Thomas wing of Baptist Hospital have reported another presence of sorts—the sounds of babies crying. Infants wailing in the hallway of a sick ward was particularly unusual, since small children—much less newborns—were not even allowed in that part of the building. Yet the crying infants were clearly heard by staff and patients on the unit at various times of the day and night.

What triggered the sounds of the wailing babies and what those sounds might mean remain a matter of conjecture. However, it is interesting to note that in traditional Christian belief, childbirth and motherhood were the special domain of Mary, the Blessed Mother. In an earlier era, infant mortality in the South was much higher than it is today. Could the sounds in question be those of deceased infants crying for the lives taken from them prematurely?

These strange and at times unnerving incidents in the wards of the old Saint Thomas building continued unabated from at least the mid-1970s into the mid-1980s.

By the eighties, however, the building, which had seen its prime in the early decades of this century, was rapidly becoming obsolete. The hospital administration, as part of its ongoing program of upgrading the quality of care, had marked the old structure for demolition to make way for new additions to the growing medical complex.

Demolition day was accompanied by the usual media hoopla. Local television stations had set up their remote units to catch the explosion for broadcast on the nightly news, and photographers and reporters from the local papers were also on hand. At the appointed time, the charges went off and the building remained standing for an instant, then collapsed like a house of cards.

I missed the television replay of the demolition on the evening news, but the following morning the daily paper had captured the event with a bird's-eye photo from a nearby rooftop. Looking closely at the photo, however, my attention was drawn to a window on the upper floor of the old building. There, at the moment of destruction, was a face staring out at the camera.

There had been no living person in the building at the time of demolition, of course; the wrecking crew had made quite sure of that. Who—or what—then, was staring out of that third-floor window? Of course, one can always say it was merely a trick of the light on the camera lens or offer some similar rationalization, but when I spoke with a number of persons familiar with the old Saint Thomas building's reputation for being haunted, or those who had experiences in its wards, they were all convinced that it was yet another, final, manifestation of Mary.

Today, a gleaming glass and steel high-rise has replaced the brick and mortar of the old Saint Thomas structure. There have been no reports, to my knowledge, of any recurrences in the new building of the strange events that set the old building apart from the ordinary. Like Elvis, Mary has left the building—for now.

22

THE GHOULS ALL GET SCARIER AT CLOSING TIME: GHOSTS AND HAUNTS OF MUSIC ROW

MUSIC CITY, USA—THE "THIRD COAST" of the entertainment world—at least that is how the pundits have come to describe the city of Nashville.

Nashville and music, especially country music, are closely linked in the public mind, and it is true that one can hardly toss a stone in any direction in this town without hitting a recording studio, music publisher, or songwriter. Nowhere in Music City do they toil harder in the rhinestone mines than on legendary Music Row, but beyond the guitar-shaped pools and the double-ended star cars lurks a darker realm that the tourists seldom see.

Unknown to the public, and often spoken of only in whispers, is the fact that unearthly entities and unseen forces share the same space with the folks who turn leaden lyrics into gold records.

During the late 1970s, when the *Urban Cowboy* craze put country music back in the limelight nationwide, a building boom of sorts hit the Row, as new companies moved in to take advantage of the fad and the more established music firms expanded into larger quarters. Then, as now, the broad boulevards and tree-lined streets of Music Row often saw brash new office buildings jostling for space with older homes. And then, as now, the Row was a place where dreams—and sometimes nightmares—can come true.

During this era on the Row, the old Schnell Mansion on Music Square East came down to make way for the new offices of Capitol Records. The peeling plaster and faded paint of the Corinthian-columned mansion gave way to the glass and brick of a modern office complex.

In due course, the staff of the music company moved into the stylish new offices and quickly settled into the daily grind of producing hit recordings. However, as the workers became familiar with their new surroundings, they began to notice strange things were happening around them.

No effort had been spared by the developers to provide first-class office accommodations, but within a short time of moving in, the new tenants began to encounter one problem after another—keys that failed to fit the new locks, doors that would close and lock all by themselves. Moreover, there seemed to be a chronic problem with the new ventilation system, which would come on and off at odd times or suddenly not work at all. The ventilation system, it seemed, had a mind of its own.

While these peculiarities, by themselves, might have been written off as simply the usual bugs in a newly constructed building, there were other things that defied simple explanations. Computers would turn on all by themselves for no apparent reason, and then, early one morning, workers arrived to find reams of computer paper rolled out on the floor—again, with no apparent cause.

Each time the computers went haywire, the office had been locked up tight for the night, and no one had come back later. Another time, a video recorder programmed to record a certain music awards show was found the next morning to have switched channels of its own accord and recorded the wrong show.

There was something else unusual about the building: The storage room exhibited an unearthly cold. Repeated efforts were made to heat the space without success. "It was just like a refrigerator in there," one worker stated, "but it was a different sort of cold—it went right through you."

Taken separately, one might have been able to dismiss the incidents as coincidence or accident. Taken together, however, it became obvious to many at Capitol and the other businesses in the building that too much was happening too often for it all to be mere chance. Many workers were convinced that supernatural forces were at work in the building.

As the strange incidents began to multiply in the weeks following the move, the possibility of having psychics inspect the structure was debated. Finally, two experienced psychics were called in to help "cleanse" the building.

Admittedly, some persons in the office were dubious about this duo of astral detectives, but after their visit, there was a noticeable decrease in the "coincidences." Whatever they did seemed to have a positive effect. At the same time, research into the background of the property on which the office building had been erected revealed a possible cause of the unearthly disturbances.

It seems that the previous owners of the land, the Schnell family, had long had a reputation in the neighborhood for their eccentric—if not positively bizarre—behavior. The patriarch of the family, Jacob Schnell, had been a plainspoken, hardworking grain merchant. For many years, he and his family had lived in an apartment over his store on Jefferson Street, in the Germantown district.

Although he was of plebeian birth, Jacob had done well for himself and had aspirations for his daughters. He wished to see his two girls accepted into polite society and wanted them to marry well.

Jacob spent a fortune building a palatial new home on the posh west side of Nashville, and when it was finished, he invited the city's social elite to the coming-out party for his daughters, Lena and Bertha. It was his version of the American Dream. What Jacob forgot, though, is that nightmares are dreams, too.

Jacob spared no expense for the fête, and on the night of the ball, the Schnell Mansion was aglow with a thousand lights. Elaborate decorations were everywhere, and the house was decorated from top to bottom with the finest furniture and fittings. Old Jacob had bought his young daughters the most beautiful gowns money could buy.

But despite all his wealth, Jacob could not buy acceptance from the "old money" set that ruled Nashville's high society. All that night, Jacob, his daughters, and the servants in their fine livery awaited the arrival of the guests—but not one person who was invited to the gala showed up.

Humiliated, the embittered Jacob moved back to his simple lodgings over his feed and grain store—but not Lena and Bertha. Jacob vowed to have his revenge on the community that had snubbed him. He ordered the two girls to remain in the new mansion, but they were to do nothing to maintain the house. Jacob wanted the house to slowly deteriorate, to become an eyesore to all the snobs in the affluent neighborhood.

Over time, the beautiful mansion went to seed, as Jacob had planned. The lawn became choked with weeds, the paint flaked and peeled but was not redone, plaster fell from the ceiling and was not repaired. After some years, the heating system finally broke down and it too was left in disrepair.

Jacob's beautiful daughters, like the mansion, also went to seed. Instead of enjoying marriage and family in the working-class neighborhood of Germantown, the two girls remained in the mansion, graying and fading as it did, turning into eccentric old spinsters.

When their father died, Lena and Bertha came into a substantial inheritance, and being thrifty like their father, they invested it wisely. The sisters were well off financially, but one could not have told it by looking at their house. Those neighbors who knew them in later years found them to be quite intelligent and savvy businesswomen—who lived like paupers in the old house.

The sisters' reputation for oddness was confirmed

when Lena died. Bertha could not bear to be parted from her sister, it seems, so she never bothered to call a funeral home to make arrangements. Lena's body remained in the house, unburied. One supposes Bertha preferred to imagine that Lena was just sleeping, although the odor in the house quickly informed one otherwise.

Bertha's bizarre behavior finally became too much for the neighbors, and they reported her to the health department. Lena was taken away and buried at last, in Mount Olivet Cemetery—ironically, side by side with the very people who had once snubbed her.

In time, Bertha followed her sister to the grave and the sad old home stood empty. Finally, the wrecking ball put an end to the house that held so many doleful memories, but the pain and suffering the house once witnessed apparently survived its demolition. Many think the malfunctions in the Capitol Records offices were the work of old Jacob, who resented the posh new quarters. Others feel the ghosts that haunt the building are the shades of the two sisters who are still dutifully trying to carry out their father's obsessive command. In either case, something uncanny has been at work on the Row.

Further up the street, where Music Row meets the rest of the world, there is a cluster of shops that cater to the tourists who come to Nashville to see the favorite haunts of the stars. In at least one of these places, however, there once were haunts of a supernatural sort.

In the late 1980s, one of the most popular watering holes in the Music Row area was Gilley's—Nashville's own version of the legendary Texas honky-tonk. Gilley's and its mechanical bull set up shop at the end of Music Row, just up the street from where Hank Williams's ranch-style house had been moved and opened for tours. Gilley's was located in a rambling Victorian house with a quaint mansard roof.

In the fall of 1989, a new arrival to Music City was working as the resident custodian and security guard for a warehouse adjacent to the honky-tonk. The new arrival was named Joey, and it was his job to keep an eye on the property and deter would-be vandals and vagrants from hanging around. Joey would soon earn his keep—and then some.

Like many newcomers to Nashville, Joey was a man of many talents—poet, producer, union organizer, boot-painter, artist, activist. At this point in time, though, Joey was simply glad to have a roof over his head and free time during the day to pursue opportunities on the Row and elsewhere.

Like the nightclub next door, the warehouse had once been a residence and dated back well into the nineteenth century. Joey had set up a cot in what had once been its kitchen, and there is where he passed his nights.

At first, Joey slept soundly in the old kitchen and paid little heed to the noises he heard in the house at night. Old buildings tend to settle, he thought, and maybe those odd noises were only that and nothing more.

But along with the creaking of the floorboards, Joey soon detected other sounds—sounds like moans and muffled cries. Even so, Joey did not take much notice, for he had recently arrived from Chicago and was used to nighttime disturbances. After all, what would be considered a riot in Nashville would seem like a slow night on the South Side to someone from Chicago.

But the more Joey tried to ignore the strange sounds, the more violent the disturbances became. One evening, for example, Joey was deep in slumber when he was abruptly brought fully awake by a loud, blood-curdling shriek. It sounded as though a woman were being savagely attacked somewhere close by—somewhere very close by—perhaps just outside in the alley.

Rushing out the door, his bowie knife in hand, Joey expected to confront some murderous maniac. He scanned the alley and the street for the attacker and victim but could see no one at all. Not a soul was on the street, and a thorough search of the area revealed no sign of any struggle.

A short time after this incident, Joey was drifting off to sleep one night when he was jolted out of his cot by a loud, sharp sound. It was as if a metal pail had been thrown off the roof and clattered down into the backyard. Again, Joey went outside to investigate, and once more he could find no one in the yard, the alley, or even on the roof. Nor was there any sign of a metal bucket.

The days passed, and as Halloween approached, Joey noticed a distinct increase in the number and intensity of incidents in and around the old building. The incidents were not just occurring at night anymore, either.

One crisp autumn afternoon, Joey was idly looking out the kitchen window, gazing at an old oak tree standing in the yard, its majestic limbs slowly shedding brightly hued leaves one by one. It was a big tree, as old or older than the buildings surrounding it.

As Joey sat contemplating the oak, something abruptly slammed into the tree with incredible force, almost as if some giant invisible fist had punched the tree trunk. The entire house and its stone foundation shook from the force of the blow. The oak tree still remained standing, but in an instant, all the leaves had been shaken to the ground.

It was at this point that Joey realized he was dealing with something far more sinister than a mischievous poltergeist. Whatever was loose in the yard, it certainly was not Casper the Friendly Ghost.

One afternoon a few days after that awesome demonstration, Joey heard strange sounds coming from the same part of the backyard. At first, it sounded like someone walking about in the leaf-covered yard, but when Joey looked out the window, he saw no one. However, as he looked and listened more closely, he realized that something was indeed out there.

The sound was akin to the noise static electricity makes when it discharges, but it was occurring in a regular rhythm—like someone walking. Peering closely at the leaf-covered yard, Joe could see oval clumps of leaves being depressed in a regular pattern around the oak, as if a pair of invisible feet were pacing round and round the tree. The eerie scene continued for some time, and it was all happening in broad daylight.

Joey was not a superstitious man, but he could not escape the conclusion that he was in the presence of something supernatural, perhaps even something demonic. At first, he assumed he was the only one experiencing these bizarre events, but as he got to know the staff at Gilley's next door, he discovered that he was far from alone in his unearthly encounters.

The Gilley's staff had also been experiencing strange events that defied logical explanation. Talking with the club's employees and management, Joe discovered that, if anything, Gilley's was even more haunted than was his warehouse. Almost every member of the staff at Gilley's had had run-ins with something they believed to be supernatural—unexplained noises and other poltergeist-like incidents—but the strange happenings at the night club were far more intense than what Joey had experienced. The Gilley's folks had encountered fully visible—and tangible—phantoms!

In some cases, the apparitions appeared dressed in Civil War era uniforms. But the ghosts at Gilley's did far more than merely appear and disappear—and they were not particularly friendly. On at least one occasion, one of the manager's sons was assaulted by one of these phantoms, and that particular "figment of the imagination" packed quite a wallop.

The old gray mansion with its mansard roof had seen many years come and go, and what horrors it had witnessed no one living could know. Fortunately for the club's customers, the malevolent spirits only seemed to appear around closing time and later.

Today, Gilley's is gone, and the urban cowboys and cowgirls have gone elsewhere to dance and find romance. But elsewhere on Music Row, there still are places where the restless dead yet abide, and even if they haven't been much in evidence of late, they still remain, watching and waiting.

23

THE PHANTOM WARRIORS
OF WESSINGTON

LONG BEFORE THE ARRIVAL OF THE WHITE
man, Indians roamed the hills and vales of the Cumberland Basin at will, reaping the bounty of the land. Like
many who came after them, they did not always abide
there in peace with one another.

Ruins of ancient forts of earth and stone stand as
mute witnesses to some great conflict of old. What tribes
built these structures and what became of them has
sparked considerable debate. What is certain, however, is
that when the whites arrived, the fertile lands of the
Cumberland were already considered taboo by the tribes
as a place to settle—it was a land sacred to all but possessed by none.

In Sumner County, the now placid meadows near
Drake's Creek were once quite literally a "dark and bloody
ground." Local tradition holds that these fields once were
the scene of a ferocious battle. So fierce and sanguinary
was the struggle that the very ground became saturated
with the blood of the dead and dying, and as the precious
fluid oozed into the creek, the stream flowed crimson.

The victors gave their honored dead a hero's funeral
on the field of battle. The enemy dead, it is said, were
mutilated and fed to the dogs.

When the bureaucrats chose this same meadow as
the site for the new county school, they may not have

known that it was hallowed ground—or if they did, they did not care. At any rate, once the bulldozers started to roll, and began unearthing Indian graves, it was too late.

Grave after grave was ripped apart, and one after another, dump trucks laden with the jumbled remains of the Old Ones rumbled away to some nameless landfill. For ages uncounted, the warriors had slumbered in peace, and now newcomers had come to disturb their rest. But if the Indians' bones had departed, their spirits had not, for even before the new school was finished, there were signs that these warriors would not go passively into the darkness.

Construction workers are not a timid sort, as a rule, so when their shovels began turning up ribs, leg bones, and leering skulls, they should not have been overly concerned. Strangely, though, the contractor soon found his workers calling in sick in unusually high numbers, while others would quit after only a few days on the job. There was more than old bones and broken pottery spooking the men—far more.

Rumors about the work site began to circulate, rumors of strange, freakish accidents and unusual incidents. The contractor kept a lid on things, hiring new men to replace the others as they quit, and eventually the job was finished. But questions remained about what had caused so many able-bodied, usually fearless men to flee the place in panic.

Wessington Elementary School opened in 1974 with the usual celebrations, and soon its hallways were echoing to the sounds of fresh young scholars. The school seemed pleasant enough; its low brick building nestled in a broad meadow near a quiet meandering stream, with woods beyond and pastures receding into distant hazy gray hills.

The school was located in a prosperous suburb of Nashville, and its bright students and dedicated staff soon earned it a reputation as being one of the better elementaries in Sumner County. But beneath this placid surface, things were much less idyllic than they seemed.

The first indications that something unusual was

afoot were minor episodes, easily ignored. For example, one Sunday the principal was alone at the school, catching up on paperwork in his office. He had left the door to the hallway open for ventilation and was so immersed in his work that he probably would not have noticed the sound at all, had not the school been so deathly quiet.

The principal thought he heard the sound of footsteps coming from the hallway. It was not loud, more like the soft padding of leather moccasins than the tapping of hard leather soles or the squeaking of sneakers on linoleum.

Wondering who might be in the building on a Sunday, and how they had gotten in, the principal went to investigate. When he looked out into the hallway, however, the sound stopped and there was no one to be seen. When the principal returned to his desk, the sound of someone walking returned.

When he checked the hallway a second time, the sound ceased and there was again no one to be seen. The principal then made a through search of the building, but the place was empty and everything was locked up tightly. Save for himself, there was no other living being in the school.

The principal was not the only one hearing things at Wessington. Faculty members reported strange sounds on occasion, and more than once the school secretary and her assistants claimed to have heard the sound of horses being watered at a brook or spring. The school's administrative offices are located in the exact middle of the building, a windowless block of rooms with no direct access to the outside, so it is virtually impossible that the sounds had filtered in from the nearby fields.

Long ago, however, on the spot where the offices are located, there was a small spring-fed brook where Indians would take their ponies for water. Did the staff hear the sounds of long-dead warriors watering their mounts?

On the north side of the school, one third grade classroom is believed to have been built over the grave of a mighty medicine man and chieftain. Several children attending Mrs. S.'s class in that room have testified that they have heard the sounds of drumbeats and a low chorus of chanting voices. Next door, in Mrs. C.'s class, students sitting on the left side of the room, closest to the Mrs. S.'s classroom, have also heard the eerie chanting and drumbeats.

Another time, two fourth grade boys were walking in the hallway on their way to class when they heard footsteps behind them. They turned to see who it was, but no one was there. When the continued down the hall, the sound of footsteps returned and became louder and faster, as if someone were trotting or jogging. As the sound drew closer and closer, the pace of the footsteps became faster and faster. Finally, the two boys felt a gust of wind, as though someone had passed them at a full run. At the same instant, the lights went out in the nearby boys restroom. As with the other incidents, there was no visible agency involved.

The strange occurrences at Wessington have not been limited to odd sounds. There have been physical manifestations, witnessed by students as well as staff. In Mrs. S.'s classroom one afternoon, for example, a huge gust of wind howled through the room, scattering papers, pencils, and projects throughout the area. What made this occurrence unusual was that there were no windows in the classroom and both the inside and outside doors were securely shut at the time.

In Miss Cathy's class one morning, students were busily engaged in their studies when an empty desk began to move all on its own. The desk moved only an inch or so, but it attracted the attention of the students sitting near it. The children were about to tell their teacher about the moving desk when, abruptly, it scooted across the floor from one side of the room to the other.

Outside of the main building in the last few years, portable classrooms have been added to handle the growing enrollment of the school. One of these classrooms is reputed to have been located directly over Indian children's graves. One day, without warning, a chair started moving across the room. A short time later the same day, another chair moved—this time pulling itself out from under a desk, as if someone were going to sit in it. It would seem that teacher had more attending her class that day than a simple head count of students could reveal.

More dramatic than these incidents was the time when Mrs. L., a resources teacher, brought a stalactite to school to show her class. She had obtained the specimen from a local cave and was intending to use it to illustrate her discussion of the area's geography. No sooner had the teacher taken out the stone for show and tell, however, than objects began falling off the walls throughout the room. A partition toppled with a crash and shelving collapsed, scattering its contents all over the floor.

At the same time, the American flag in the classroom began waving, as if in a strong breeze—yet all the doors were shut tight. It was only when the stalactite was removed from the classroom that the violent demonstrations ceased.

What could have set off such a dramatic display? Skeptics might dismiss the unusual activity as being the result of a minor earthquake or tremor. But aside from the fact that there hasn't been an earthquake in the Mid-South for nearly two hundred years, no other classroom at Wessington experienced similar disturbances that day.

Rather, it seems far more likely in this case that an *un*earthly agency was involved than any sort of natural earthly event. A number of caves dot the Cumberland basin, and in many of them, mummified remains have been found. These do not seem to have been normal Indian burials, and scientists have failed to explain why or how the mummies came to be there. It is widely believed, however, that they are the bodies of powerful medicine men—sorcerers who regarded the caves as places of power resonating with magic. It could well be that the teacher had collected the stalactite unwittingly from one such place of power, and when she displayed the stone on the hallowed ground upon which Wessington was built, its presence disturbed whatever spirits may reside there.

Other incidents at Wessington, seemingly of a mundane nature, may also have a supernatural aspect to them. Take the case of vandalism in Mrs. R's kindergarten class, for example. One morning, Mrs. R. discovered that the glass panel on the exterior door to her classroom had been broken, perhaps by vandals. The police were summoned and conducted an investigation, which uncovered some peculiar facts.

Oddly, nothing was missing from the room, and the only thing that had actually been damaged was the glass panel on the outside door. As the police examined the area around the door, they could find no evidence that a brick or knife had been used to break the glass. The only thing they did find that might have done such damage was a stone arrowhead—certainly large and sharp enough to shatter glass if had it been launched from a bow. The police, of course, dismissed that theory—how could such a thing be?—and the case remained unsolved.

Perhaps the most dramatic incident at Wessington occurred only a few years ago. One morning, as the students were hard at work at their lessons, and counting the minutes till lunchtime, the public address system began to boom out an announcement.

What seemed to be the voice of the school principal announced that school was being dismissed. The abrupt announcement struck everyone, students and teachers alike, as odd. It was a perfectly sunny day, and there seemed to be no reason for an early dismissal. One teacher, Mrs. C., went to the office to see what was going on. Arriving there, she ran into Mrs. P., the school secretary, who had just arrived from a county board of education meeting in Gallatin.

The teacher asked why the principal was closing school so early—the teachers had not been informed of any half-day sessions. The secretary replied that the principal could not possibly have made such an announcement, even had he wished to do so, because she had left him at the meeting in Gallatin a half-hour ago, and he had been there all morning!

The principal was not prone to practical jokes, nor was he in the building when the strange announcement was made. He was never known to record announcements, and in any event, the public address system did not have the capability to do timed playbacks. The entire school had heard his voice, or something that closely resembled it—yet no one had come or gone from the principal's office all morning.

While searching the principal's office for intruders, the only thing out of the ordinary that was found was an old shoe—a moccasin, to be exact. Some months later, a visiting expert from the science museum in Nashville was making a presentation to one of the classes and took a look at the odd footwear. The expert declared that the moccasin was an ancient and very rare Indian artifact. No one dared give voice to the thought, but most everyone in the classroom knew that the moccasin had belonged to the mysterious intruder—an Indian warrior, perhaps dead a thousand years!

Since that incident, the school has continued to experience minor incidents on a regular basis: Lights go out in the bathrooms for no reason; students in the hallway hear odd noises even though all the doors are closed; books in the library fall off the shelves by themselves; the principal finds a note on his desk written in some ancient script. And so it goes; such incidents have become too mundane to even bother reporting.

So far, no one has been injured during the strange happenings at Wessington Elementary. Apparently, the phantom warriors that haunt the nearby meadows are not malevolent, they are just disturbed at what has happened to their happy hunting ground.

Officially, of course, none of this ever happened. On the record, county officials have denied that any of these incidents have any basis in fact. The same is true of reports coming from the former Hendersonville High School—now Ellis Middle School—which was built on a pioneer graveyard. Although the bureaucrats refuse to say anything on the record, what they say in private to one another about these hauntings is another matter entirely.

Regardless of official denials, Indian spirits have inhabited the Dark and Bloody Ground for millennia, the white man but a few centuries. It remains to be seen who will last longer.

24

TENNESSEE'S
HAUNTED CAPITOL

AS A RULE, ABOUT THE ONLY STRANGE
beings that haunt the hallways of a state legislature are
lobbyists looking for political favors, and the only spirits
you will find there are eighty proof. In Tennessee, however, the hallowed halls of politics are haunted by spirits
of a more spectral sort.

Since well before the Civil War, the Tennessee State
Capitol in Nashville has crowned the summit of the city.
Sitting high atop a steep bluff, its majestic many-
columned halls and classical lines easily bring to mind
the famed Acropolis in Athens, Greece. And just as ancient Athens was the birthplace of democracy, Nashville
was the birthplace of Jacksonian democracy. It was, perhaps, for these reasons that Nashville became known as
the "Athens of the South."

But if the spirit of democracy lingers in the venerable halls of the Tennessee State Capitol, so do other spirits.

The story of the capitol's ghosts is linked closely
with the history of the building itself. In the early days,
Knoxville was the capital of the state, and Nashville lay
on the edge of the howling wilderness. But as the state
grew, and the population moved west, it made sense to
have a more centralized location for the capital—and
Nashville eventually was selected for that honor.

At first, the state legislature met in a small building—some called it a hovel—in town. But the legislators realized that they needed a suitable place with enough space to conduct the affairs of state. Land was purchased on the summit of the bluff known as Cedar Knob overlooking the town of Nashville. This plot of land had a commanding view of the countryside and city, a promising beginning for the new capitol building.

In 1845, William Strickland, a highly respected architect from Philadelphia, was retained to design and construct the new building. Strickland moved to Nashville, thinking the project would take but a few years to finish. He stayed nine years—dying before ever seeing the project completed.

One reason for the delays in construction, apparently, was a chronic shortage of funds. When it came to paying for their grand new capitol, the legislature, it seems, was quite tight with the purse strings. Strickland's own salary was constantly in arrears, and extracting money from the politicians for building materials and labor proved to be harder than delivering a breech-birth calf—a cow would howl a lot less than the legislators did, for one thing.

In addition to chronic money problems, Strickland also had to contend with Samuel Morgan. Appointed by the legislature to the Capitol Commission, it was Morgan's mission to oversee Strickland's construction of the building. To say that the two men did not see eye to eye would be a bit of an understatement. If Strickland thought blue would be a suitable color for a wall, Morgan would say gray. If William wanted marble for the stairways, Sam would tell him limestone was good enough. If one wanted a smooth finish on the outside stone, the other insisted on a rough finish—and so it went.

Many are the times the two men would get into heated—and loud—arguments right at the construction site, haggling over details of the building's construction. It's a wonder the two men never came to blows. Duels had been fought over considerably less.

When William Strickland died in April 1854, the

state voted to construct a vault within the walls of the capitol in which to inter his body, "in honor of his genius in erecting so grand a work." Strickland was laid to rest in a spot of his own choosing—on the northeast wall of the north portico, at basement level.

This was indeed a rare honor the state accorded Strickland. In fact, in its entire history, the State of Tennessee has honored just one other man in such a manner: none other than Sam Morgan.

So it came to pass that William Strickland's contrary overseer was interred within the same walls as he, the two sharing the close quarters of their limestone resting place for eternity. Therein, it seems, lies the problem, for the two men entombed together till doomsday have never stopped arguing.

Today, in addition to state legislators and their staffs, the capitol is regularly visited by innumerable school groups and charter tours, but very few of these people are aware of any spectral presence on the hill. At night, however, it is a different story. Everyone leaves the building except for the maintenance crews, while state troopers and the Capitol Police guard the grounds throughout the night. A number of these government night workers have had repeated experiences with the ghosts of Capitol Hill.

Not long ago, two new officers had just been assigned to the night shift, with the responsibility of patrolling the capitol grounds. One, a state trooper, patrolled the area in a distinctive black and tan Caprice cruiser; the other, a member of the Capitol Police, made his rounds in a white Lumina with red and blue stripes, and the state logo blazoned in red on the side.

The area around Capitol Hill is normally quiet at night, although drunks and vagrants sometimes hang out there, and there is an occasional rowdy disturbance to break the monotony of a long shift. So it did not strike one of the new officers as terribly strange when, one night around 9:00 P.M., he heard a loud argument while patrolling the hill. Halting his white patrol car, he called for backup before proceeding to investigate.

In short order, a black and tan cruiser pulled up next

to him, and the two officers got out of their cars and approached the area of the grounds from which the disturbance seemed to be coming.

Although floodlights illuminate the capitol at night, there are a number of places in the shadows around its base where an assailant might lurk. The two officers proceeded cautiously, making a circuit around the base of the building. When they came to the north side—the direction from which the sounds seemed to be coming—they could find nothing.

They made a thorough search of the area, beaming their flashlights into every nook and corner, but could find no one. This was most curious, since the sounds of the disturbance had been loud and quite nearby—and the culprits did not have time to get away.

The following night, the same Capitol Police officer was making his nightly rounds. At 9 P.M., he again heard the sounds of two men engaged in a violent argument, yelling and cursing at each other in a most heated manner. Again, per regulations, the policeman called for assistance before investigating. Once more, the state trooper was the closest officer to the scene and arrived to provide backup. And, like the previous night, when the two checked the area, there was no one to be found. It was the same story on many ensuing nights.

At first, the officers were disturbed and bewildered by these odd occurrences on their new beat, until some veteran patrolmen explained it all to them. Other troopers and Capitol Police officers had experienced the same phenomenon off and on for years. For some reason, the sounds always began around 9 P.M., when a loud argument would erupt—seemingly in the area of the north foundation wall-and continue for several minutes. When officers investigated, no one was ever found.

Others on the night shift had become used to the strange quarrels and paid them little heed anymore. The voices, they told the new officers, were those of the capitol's architects, still arguing over the design!

While unusual in its own right, this recurring incident was not the only strange happening to occur near William Strickland's tomb. One day, as another trooper was driving slowly around the access road running just below Strickland's tomb, he saw someone toss a stone in the direction of the tomb. The stone seemed to stop in midair and then drop to the ground—almost as if someone had grabbed it in flight.

Several years before this, a security officer on duty one night inside the capitol building had fallen asleep in the library. He was awakened by a tap on his shoulder. Thinking it was his partner who had finished making his rounds, the man turned around to look but saw no one.

Being quite tired, the officer started to nod off again, and once more he was awakened by a tap on the shoulder. This happened three times—each time the officer awoke with a start, only to find no one else in the room.

In 1987, a similar incident occurred to some maintenance workers in the building. The crew had been repainting the offices and hallways on the capitol's second floor and was working late in order to finish the job on time. Two of the men went out for dinner, leaving a third locked inside the building. The lone painter decided to catch twenty winks on one of the antique Victorian couches in the area where he was working.

The man was sound asleep when someone knocked his feet off the couch. Startled, he sat up, thinking his two partners were back, but no one was there. The painter lay back down, but no sooner had he done so than his feet were again shoved off the couch. Looking up, he stared into the eyes of a bearded man wearing a Confederate uniform!

The gray ghost spoke to him in a commanding tone, saying, "Young man, keep your feet off the couch!" The maintenance worker has not been back to that second-floor office since.

Other witnesses tell of a gossamer-like phantom floating about the capitol's tower. The tower has been closed to the public for years, but workers have reported seeing a wispy sort of apparition there on a number of occasions.

During the Civil War, some Yankee soldiers had shot and killed a state legislator on the steps of the tower. The story goes that the man was a Confederate sympathizer blocking the soldiers' way to prevent them from raising the Union flag over the capitol. They shot him dead, and now his restless shade still hovers about the steep stairwell that leads to the topmost turret of the capitol, the place where the flagpole is mounted.

At times, other workers have claimed to have seen the ghost of Rachel Jackson haunting the governor's offices. In the 1980s, during the administration of Governor Ned Ray McWherter, a portrait of Rachel hung in the offices of Jim Kennedy, the governor's chief of staff. Maintenance workers on a number of occasions have claimed to have seen the late Mrs. Jackson, all clad in white, floating through the governor's suite late at night.

Over the years, a host of hauntings have been reported in the old building and surrounding grounds—the foregoing are but a few of the better documented ones. At other times, people have heard the sounds of barking dogs that aren't there or have seen locked doors suddenly open of their own accord.

It is said that politics makes strange bedfellows, and the Tennessee State Capitol has certainly given new meaning to that phrase. It's enough to make one wonder just how much Halloween might be lurking within the hallowed halls of state.

25

THE HAUNTING OF BREEZE HILL

"The distinction between past, present and future is only an illusion, however persistent."

—Albert Einstein

SOME HOUSES ARE MERELY AN ASSEM-blage of wood and plaster that provide shelter from the storm and nothing more. Other houses, even from the first, seem to be more than just physical constructs—much more.

These latter dwellings possess personalities all their own, reflecting the collective experiences—good and bad—of those who have lived there. At times, it may seem as though such a house is a living entity. Nashville's Breeze Hill Mansion is one of those places.

Even in its period of decline, the antebellum mansion looked majestic, standing tall on the crest of Breeze Hill, overlooking the old Franklin Pike and the sparkling waters of Brown's Creek. For more than one hundred fifty years the venerable structure withstood the batterings of man, nature, and time—and, until the very end, endured them all.

Breeze Hill was built in the early 1800s by Joseph Vaulx, a veteran of the American Revolution who had come west from North Carolina to settle after the war.

When the house was completed in 1832, it was one of the grandest homes in Davidson County, and the Vaulx plantation soon became a showplace of the Mid-South.

The Vaulx family had prospered in the years before the Civil War, but the conflict that pitted brother against brother brought hard times to the family as well as to the house in which it dwelled. Overlooking a major road southward, the mansion saw the march and countermarch of armies and was occupied by both sides at various times during the war. Yankee foragers stole the family's crops and livestock at will, and while the Confederates paid for the goods they took, their paper money was worthless.

During the battle of Nashville in 1864, Breeze Hill was right in the center of the Confederate lines. At one point, the mansion was used as a headquarters and hospital, and untold numbers of maimed and mangled men died of their wounds while lying on the surrounding grounds.

During the battle, the Confederate headquarters received an unexpected visitor. A woman arrived on horseback seeking help; she had injured her foot in a riding accident, she said, and asked if the southern gentlemen might be of assistance. The young lady was immediately granted sanctuary by the officers and was assisted up the tall, winding staircase to an upstairs bedroom, where she could rest her injured appendage.

Later that evening, the Rebel commanders were downstairs in the drawing room, reviewing plans for the upcoming engagement. They were engrossed in their discussion when a high-pitched shriek rang out, followed by the sound of an object crashing down out in the hallway. The officers rushed into the hall to find, at the foot of the winding stairs, the lifeless form of the young woman, her neck broken.

The mysterious lady who had arrived at their doorstep turned out to be a Yankee spy. She had been leaning over the railing on the staircase, trying to hear what the officers were saying, when she lost her balance and tumbled down the staircase to her doom.

Scenes of death were not unique at Breeze Hill in those days, and the tides of war left their scars on the house and its inhabitants. The Vaulx family lived in Nashville for a number of years after the war but only occasionally visited the place. The last Vaulx family member, son Joseph, died within the mansion's walls in 1908.

For a time, the house stood empty, and as the grounds became neglected and overgrown, the place took on a sinister aspect. It was about this time that the mansion began to acquire a reputation for being haunted.

In the 1920s, Morris Wilson bought the estate and made extensive renovations. Breeze Hill once more became a place of gaiety and mirth as the Wilsons held numerous parties there, some of which lasted for days on end. In 1938, Morris's only child, Elizabeth, inherited the house—and everything within it.

Elizabeth married one William Scribner, and the couple continued to live in her ancestral home. While they were happy there for many years, spectral encounters of one sort or another had become regular occurrences.

One time, Elizabeth entered a room and found her husband talking to himself. She asked him who he was conversing with—whereupon he answered that he'd been talking to her. When Elizabeth informed him that she had just that second entered the room, the startled Mr. Scribner replied, "Then who was that who came in and sat down behind me fifteen minutes ago?"

One morning, the couple watched as a female ghost materialized right before them and began moving in their direction. The spirit walked right through a desk in the room, stayed for a few seconds, and then vanished into thin air. On another occasion, a visiting houseguest was awakened in the middle of the night by something brushing against him as he lay in bed.

Once, after the Scribners had vacated the house for good, a woman caretaker reported that she had awakened one cold winter morning to find quilts stacked over her on the bed and a blazing fire going in the fireplace. The trouble was that neither her nor her associates had lit the fire or taken out the quilts!

Such occurrences became all too frequent during the time the Scribners lived at Breeze Hill. Elizabeth and William had grown used to entities climbing the stairs, doorknobs turning on their own, and the spectral sound of jingling spurs, but keeping good help on staff proved to be a bit of a problem.

For reasons best known to the family, the Scribners moved out of the Breeze Hill Mansion in 1961. Although Mrs. Scribner remained fond of the home in which she had lived for so many years, she never again crossed its threshold.

Over the next decade or so, the Scribners retained different caretakers to maintain the house and grounds, but often as not, they proved to be rather careless as caretakers. Vandals came in at random and looted or destroyed things; professional art thieves made several large-scale raids on the house, carrying off truckloads of valuable antiques and documents. During the course of the sixties, hippies at one point turned it into a crash pad, lighting fires on the floor to keep warm and using antique furniture as kindling.

The Vaulx estate was in sorry shape by the early seventies, when three friends started a quest to save the historic home. John Bell, Robert Bolanger, and Wayne Bottoms were three enterprising young men who shared an affection for old things.

Apparently, Mrs. Scribner had approached Bell as early as 1967 for assistance in preserving Breeze Hill, but it was not until May 1973 that Bell and his companions were able to do anything. With youthful enthusiasm, the trio set about repairing the effects of more than a decade of neglect and abuse, recruiting anyone and everyone who was willing to help.

But, as Breeze Hill's previous residents had discovered, the trio soon found they were not the mansion's only inhabitants—even if they were the only living ones.

At odd times, the men would hear a loud sound

coming from the winding staircase, almost as if a heavy object were tumbling down its length. Running to investigate, they would be unable to find anything. At other times, they saw an apparition called the Gray Lady.

When they described these close encounters, the Scribners told the men the story of the female Yankee spy and her untimely demise. She apparently was the Gray Lady, and the female phantom was frequently sighted not only by the trio but also by a number of visitors. As Bell and the others became more familiar with the house, it became apparent that it was haunted by more than just the Gray Lady—far more.

In one instance, a guest came in through the front door and stood in the main hall for a moment, peering out a nearby window at the front lawn. In an instant, the scene changed, and instead of an urban Nashville landscape, the man found himself looking at tall shade trees and horsedrawn carriages that were pulling up in front of the house. People dressed in elaborate antebellum dresses and ruffled shirts were dismounting from the carriages, apparently arriving for a cotillion.

The visitor's flashback in time lasted a full five minutes and was complete in every detail. He no doubt began to wonder if he would ever be able to get back to his own time. But when his time warp—or vision—finally ended, the terrified guest fled the premises, vowing never to return to Breeze Hill again.

John Bell, as well, had flashbacks to the antebellum period, though none quite so elaborate or lengthy as the one related above. From time to time, he would experience brief one- or two-second glimpses of another time— apparently of the golden era before the Civil War, when the house was in its full glory.

These visions of another time were what psychic researchers refer to as "retrocognition"—the phenomenon of experiencing or "seeing" another period in time—in this case, a previous era of the house itself. It is difficult to say for sure whether these gentlemen were really experiencing another era or if they perhaps were in some sort of trance induced by spirits inhabiting the mansion.

But these were not the only strange tricks with time that Breeze Hill played.

The house had a knack of somehow distorting the passage of time—or at least one's perception of it. The residents of the mansion, and virtually anyone else who stayed there for any duration, often had an uncanny sense of time somehow being out of place—perhaps that it was even standing still. Clocks and watches brought into Breeze Hill for more than a brief span would almost invariably be found to run slow, fast—or not at all.

There were physical manifestations inside the house, in addition to the perceptual distortions. Oil paintings mounted in heavy and ornate antique frames were often found to have been carefully lifted off the wall and gently placed on the floor, or sometimes moved into another room entirely.

At first, Bell and the others thought the spirits they were encountering were harmless, even benign. No doubt some of them were, but the trio soon had experiences that led them to believe there were other entities in the house that were not so friendly. There was most definitely a dark side to the haunting of Breeze Hill.

The resident phantoms seemed well disposed toward Bell himself, but in one instance, one of the other two men was standing at the head of the stairs when he was pushed by unseen hands. Had he not caught himself on the banister, the man very well may have broken his neck and died—much as the pretty Yankee spy had done more than a century before.

At other times, "shapeless entities," rather than human-like ghosts, were seen flying across the room, and the young adventurers instinctually could sense that these nameless horrors were somewhat less than amiable in their relations with mortals.

All this added up to considerably more than a few lost souls that had become unstuck in time. Both of John Bell's friends moved out of the house after the shoving incident. Bell, although alarmed at these turns of events, was still powerfully attracted to the house and remained dedicated to its preservation.

After several years as the custodian and erstwhile curator at the mansion, Bell married, and while he wished to continue his quest, he had become concerned for the safety of his growing family. What is one to do when disembodied spirits infest one's home? Deadbeat tenants can be evicted, poor relations can be sent home, and an exterminator can always be called in for termites or rodents, but ghosts and unclean spirits are another matter entirely. Who ya' gonna call? In this case, a lady named Mildred Cowan.

At first glance, Mildred Cowan would have seemed an unlikely candidate for "ghostbuster." Instead of some bug-eyed psychic with unruly hair and a thick accent, Mrs. Cowan projected the image of a dignified and cultured society matron.

Born into a prominent Nashville family and marrying well, Mildred for many years had lived the conventional life of a proper southern lady, serving on charitable boards and being active in cultural organizations. But one day in 1965, she had an experience that turned her life around.

A close friend came to visit that day, which was not unusual except that Mildred knew the man had died the day before. His ghost said nothing, but there was no mistaking his appearance. Mildred took this as a sign that she had been given a higher calling in life.

As time went by, people began asking Mildred's help in ridding their homes of unwanted "visitors." Most of these folks would not have been caught dead at a séance or similar affair, but they could not ignore the fact that their homes were haunted. And Mildred discovered that she was quite good at "cleansing" such houses.

So it was that John Bell and his wife approached Mildred to do a similar cleansing of Breeze Hill. On the appointed day, Mildred came to the house to perform the ritual. No weird chanting or dancing or odd new age ceremonies were employed; Mildred's methods were the epitome of orthodoxy. Using a text approved by the Anglican Church, she recited prayers from a Requiem Mass, a ritual intended to put the souls of the departed to rest.

Mildred went through Breeze Hill, reciting the prayers, armed with boxwood and holy water, and making the sign of the cross on the windows in every room. From time to time, Mildred extemporized, talking to the spirits directly and calling on God and his angels to help the lost souls rest peacefully.

After scouring the house and invoking the resident spirits to depart, Mildred left. It remained to be seen whether her cleansing had been successful. She made no guarantees, but Mildred's success rate had been one hundred percent successful thus far. In the days following her visit, the Bells kept a weather eye about the house to see if their spectral neighbors were still around.

Nothing seemed different at first. There were no dramatic incidents, but the Bells sensed that the aura pervading the house, the "enchantment" it was under, still remained. Then, one evening a few days after Mildred's visit, John Bell was awakened in the wee hours of the morning. It was about 3 A.M. and pitch dark, but he could see a light in the vestibule.

Coming fully awake, Bell realized this was no natural light and got out of bed to investigate. Entering the room, he was amazed to see a large cylindrical column of light extending from floor to ceiling and illuminating the entire area.

As Bell stood there, stunned at the sight before him, the light began to change. The blinding pillar of light started to flicker, much like a candle would. The yellow light wavered in this manner for about twenty seconds or so and then suddenly went out, as if someone had switched it off.

Bell somehow sensed that the mysterious light he had seen marked the final appearance of the spirits that had been haunting the house. Then and there, he knew his prayers had been answered.

In the ensuing days, nothing unusual happened—the first time nothing untoward had happened since the Bells had moved into the house. Whatever it was that

Mildred Cowan had done, it evidently worked. Friends who visited the house after the cleansing noticed a distinct difference. With the spirits gone, it seemed as though the mansion was no longer the nexus of some time warp; the clocks worked perfectly, and the passage of time was no different inside the house than outside. Breeze Hill, it seems, had rejoined the rest of the world.

Ironically, Mildred Cowan's cleansing of Breeze Hill may have worked too well. Now that the forces which had kept the mansion out of the normal march of time were gone, the house had a lot of catching up to do. Breeze Hill began to deteriorate at an alarming rate: Ceilings began to cave in, plaster started flaking off the walls in large sections, and the entire structure seemed to be going rapidly to seed.

John Bell and his friends had put much time and money into preserving the mansion for posterity, but by the early eighties, the Scribner family had grown tired of trying to maintain the aging house. Developers and banks were applying pressure to clear the site for more lucrative ventures, and as often happens, the bulldozers won out over those who sought to preserve their heritage.

By 1983, Breeze Hill Mansion had gone the way of the ghosts that once inhabited it. No reports of hauntings have come from the homes erected on the ground it once occupied, so one may hope the phantoms of Breeze Hill have gone for good. Still, if I were to reside on that hill overlooking the old Franklin Pike and the sparkling waters of Brown's Creek, I would make sure I always had a spray of boxwood and a bottle of holy water by my night table. Wouldn't you?

26

ADELICIA ACKLEN: THE PHANTOM BELLE OF BELMONT

WHERE TODAY MUSIC INDUSTRY MOGULS wheel and deal, buying and selling country stars like so much meat on the hoof, blooming fields of cotton and herds of livestock once held sway. Now part of the fabled Music Row district of Nashville, these city streets were once part of the equally fabled Belmont estates.

No romantic fiction could ever equal the true life story of the mistress of Belmont, Adelicia Acklen. In the golden years before the Civil War, this steel magnolia parlayed a not inconsiderable patrimony, through matrimony, into a vast agricultural empire. And the seat of her empire was the opulent Belmont Mansion.

From the time construction was first begun in the 1850s to the present day, Belmont Mansion has seen many changes—but the will and personality of Adelicia Acklen left an indelible impression on it. Adelicia's spirit is present not only in the charm and grace of the palatial dwelling's decor and design but also as a ghost which haunts the mansion's hallowed halls.

While the male of the species sought the path to power by means of the battlefield and the smoke-filled back room, Adelicia Acklen's rise to power was through the marriage bed and the ballroom. It was on these play-

ing fields that Adelicia excelled, and her real-life manip-
ulation of the male of the species would have made the
fictional Scarlet O'Hara seem like a naive schoolgirl by
comparison.

During the Civil War, for example, when Adelicia's
cotton crops in Louisiana were threatened with destruction, Adelicia traveled hundreds of miles through a lawless, war-torn no man's land. Using all of her charm and
feminine wiles, she persuaded both sides to spare her
cotton, then convinced the Rebels to provide a cavalry
escort for the Yankee wagon train she had contracted to
carry the cotton to the Union-held port of New Orleans!

It seemed as though everything Adelicia came in
contact with turned to gold for her. Other plantation
owners emerged bankrupt by the War, but Adelicia, wid-
owed for the second time, emerged as one of the richest
women in the South. And as her wealth grew, she put
more and more of it into her fabulous home on a hill outside Nashville.

In its glory days, the opulence and glamour of Belmont—and its enchanting mistress—awed even the most
jaded observers. Nor was Adelicia one to hide her light
under a basket: Elaborate ornamental gardens, imported
classical statuary, a menagerie and a zoo, even a private
bowling alley—these and more graced the grounds of
Belmont.

The balls and cotillions Adelicia held at the plantation were the talk of the South. Always scheduled during
a full moon, the galas did not begin until eleven at night
and always lasted till dawn. Adelicia was always the
center of attention, holding court in the latest Parisian
gown, while the grounds of her fabulous estate were decorated like a fairyland, with hundreds of Japanese
lanterns and the sounds of music and laughter everywhere.

Although wealth flowed through her hands like
water, Adelicia's life was not without tragedy. She lost
several of her children to disease, including two infant
twins who died within days of one another at Belmont

Mansion. It is said that she never quite recovered from the shock of losing those twins.

When Adelicia died in 1887, the mansion and the rest of her estate was sold—but the legend remained. Eventually, the mansion was turned into an exclusive girl's finishing school and for many years educated many of the nation's leading women. It placed a strong emphasis in the arts, and entertainers such as Mary Martin and Sara Ophelia Cannon, "Cousin Minnie Pearl," were counted among its alumnae.

In the 1950s, Belmont became a four-year college under the patronage of the Southern Baptist Convention, and it has retained its reputation for academic excellence to this day.

No one knows for sure when the ghost of Adelicia Acklen first was seen inside Belmont Mansion, but reports of her ghostly presence there have been circulating for decades at least. Why Adelicia would return to bedevil students and faculty at the university is something of a mystery—since her life was one that seemed to be perennially charmed with good fortune. Some say, however, that all the glamour and gaiety of what seemed a charmed life was a mask hiding an inner sadness.

Adelicia had six children with Joseph Acklen, and the loss of the twins—Laura and Corinne—was a particularly heart-rending blow. Some say that, after their deaths, whenever Adelicia walked into their bedroom at Belmont, the sound of their childish laughter would still echo in her ears. This, they say, is why she remains.

Those less sympathetic to "Addie" say that when the iron-willed mistress of Belmont realized she couldn't take the estate with her into the afterlife, she chose to stay among the mansion and its possessions.

Either way, for many years now, the strange occurrences at Belmont College—known today as Belmont University—have generally been attributed to the actions of Adelicia Acklen's ghost.

It would seem that Adelicia's genteel upbringing and polite manners have precluded Addie from being one of the rowdier sorts of spirits. She makes her presence known in subtler ways.

One time, for example, a male student was helping to prepare the old mansion for a special holiday event. In connection with the school celebration, he was stationed on the building's main staircase, high up in a section unused for many years. This area was just above where Adelicia's bedroom had once been.

As he waited all alone in the semi-darkness for his friends, the young man suddenly felt something—it was as if someone had brushed against him. Looking about, he saw no one. Returning to his station, he again felt a gentle but distinct presence, as though a person was passing him on the stairs. Several more times this happened as he waited on the stairs. The student had no doubt that it was Adelicia he felt pass him on the stairs.

Interviews with other Belmont students and alumni reveal similar experiences, and indicate a pattern of sorts. While the ghost of Adelicia Acklen roams the mansion year round, she seems particularly active at Christmastime.

Former students often tell of encounters with her during the preparations for the school's Yuletide Hanging of the Green ceremony. To the accompaniment of a large choral group singing Christmas carols, students in Dickensian fashions descend the main stairway—a broad and winding affair—by candlelight and, with much pomp and ceremony, bedeck the large Christmas tree erected in the main hall of the mansion. It is an impressive ceremony, as anyone who has witnessed it can attest, and much effort is expended by the students in preparing for the event. Many encounters with Adelicia have revolved around this particular ceremony.

In one instance, a girl was working on the program while in the Ladies Meeting Room—just below Adelicia's bedroom. As the girl concentrated on preparations for the Christmas event, she heard footsteps in the room above. The sound continued for quite some time, and it sounded for all the world like a woman was walking back and forth from Adelicia's wardrobe on one side of the room to her dressing table on the other. When searched, of course, the bedroom was found to be completely empty.

Male students posted to guard the costumes and equipment the night before the pageant have similarly reported seeing and hearing things in the same section of the house.

Reports by students of strange occurrences go back decades, but for the most part, the faculty and staff have been silent with regard to anything relating to Addie's ghostly doings. This may simply be due to a lack of encounters, although some say it is more likely due to an official attitude that such talk is frowned on and regarded as unchristian activity.

One former staff member, however, Mrs. Moore, was not hesitant to complain about the ghostly presence in the mansion. Mrs. Moore was a mature woman, experienced and worldly, not easily frightened, and certainly not given to fantasies.

One of the perks of her position with the school was that she could board for free on campus. Mrs. Moore had an apartment just off the main hall of the mansion, adjacent to what at one time had been the ballroom.

Unlike the majority of the faculty and staff, Mrs. Moore was familiar with Adelicia's home by both night and day. Apparently, she and Addie did not get along, for Mrs. Moore was continually complaining about the "noises in the night." They were more than just an occasional nuisance, apparently.

The nightly disturbances by Adelicia's (and perhaps other) ghosts caused Mrs. Moore to complain about them to nearly everyone on campus. Unable to get a whole night's sleep because of the haunting, Mrs. Moore finally moved out.

Perhaps the most dramatic incident cited as evidence of Adelicia Acklen's continuing presence at Belmont was the incident of the mantle clock. Like the timepiece in the old song, the clock supposedly had ceased to function the day that Joseph Acklen died. By tradition, however, it was believed that if one placed the clock on the mantle in Joseph Acklen's sitting room, it would begin ticking again and keep perfect time unless removed from the room.

Some years ago, a young man attending Belmont got the notion of placing the clock on the mantle and then photographing it ticking. It would be a nice photo for the college annual. In due course, he placed the clock on the mantle and, sure enough, the clock began to tick. He snapped a photo of the clock working and sent it to the developer. When the prints came back, however, he was astonished to discover that not only was the clock working but there was the figure of a woman in the photograph as well.

The woman was standing to the right of the mantle; she was tall and wearing a hooded cloak. No such person had been in the room when the young man snapped the photo, and neither the negative nor the print had been retouched in any way.

During the 1960s, some coeds were up after lights out, studying for exams. They were busy reviewing notes in a small study lounge located behind the main part of Acklen Hall, in a part of the original mansion. They had gotten permission to stay up after curfew and were engrossed in their studies.

Then they saw her—a beautiful woman dressed all in white. She had on a long, flowing gown, loosely tied at the waist, and long black hair. The woman possessed a radiant sort of beauty and appeared to be both real and solid—not some gray gossamer phantom.

The coeds sat there awestruck. By the time they recovered their wits enough to chase after the apparition, the woman in white had disappeared completely. Needless to say, when the students told school officials of the incident the next day, they did not take the girls' report seriously.

There also have been persons from outside the college community who have occasionally seen Adelicia.

As part of its ongoing commitment to preserving the old mansion and its proud history, the university has, for some years now, brought in artisans and conservators to help restore the mansion room by room to much of its former glory. Those working on the restoration have, from time to time, reported ghostly encounters that have been attributed to the spectral presence of the mistress of Belmont.

In particular, the people involved in the restoration of Adelicia's bedroom have reported strange occurrences that are generally ascribed to the room's former resident. Every time work got underway in the room, something always seemed to happen. In one notable instance, an entire wall collapsed, ruining the workman's tools.

In another case, a member of the Historic Belmont Auxiliary whose daughter was a student at the college spent the night in a guest room while engaged in restoration work there. The room was located behind the old ballroom, and during the night, the woman was awakened by noises coming from that room. She heard the unmistakable sound of teacarts being pulled across the ballroom floor and the repeated rustling of long hoopskirts. The volunteer was a woman of some breeding and education, not prone to superstition, but she could not deny the evidence of her own senses.

The ghostly echoes of a cotillion from long ago, a haunted clock, brushes with the unknown at Yuletide, and assorted other close encounters—for generations these and countless other incidents have provided proof to students—if any proof were needed—that the spirit of Adelicia Acklen, the phantom Belle of Belmont, yet dwells within their school's hallowed haunted halls.

27

THE CASE OF THE
COMBUSTIBLE PROFESSOR

PROFESSOR JAMES HAMILTON WAS A
mild-mannered man. As a mathematics instructor at the
University of Nashville, he did not have a reputation for
being a fiery lecturer, nor did he in any way have an ex-
plosive temperament. It was doubly unusual, then, when
he burst into flames one day.

The facts of the case are straightforward and clear,
but making sense of them is not so easy. Professor Hamilton's harrowing brush with the unknown, however one
may explain it, nevertheless constitutes an important
chapter in the annals of the strange phenomenon known
as spontaneous human combustion.

Nashville in the early 1800s was a brash little boom
town. Within the space of a generation, it had gone from
an outpost on the edge of the wilderness to a prosperous
city on a hill. Billing itself as the "Athens of the West,"
by 1835 Nashville had become one of the main centers of
commerce and industry west of the Appalachians, had
sent its favorite son to the White House, and had aspirations of becoming a national center of learning and culture.

The University of Nashville was originally called
Davidson Academy and had begun in a one-room stone
blockhouse—stone to make it proof against Indian attack.
Within the span of a few years, the school had grown into

a chartered four-year institution of higher learning. By 1835, its walls were rising majestically on Rutledge Hill, just south of the city, an ambitious attempt to garner credibility as a cultural center.

Also by that time, James Hamilton was a professor of mathematics, astronomy, and natural philosophy at the university. Like the school's founder, Professor Hamilton had been educated at Princeton.

January 5, 1835, dawned cold and clear in Nashville. The temperature stood at eight degrees above freezing as Professor Hamilton walked the three-quarters of a mile from his lodgings to the university, where he mounted the steps to his recitation room. Professor Hamilton remained there with his class of young scholars until eleven o'clock in the forenoon, at which time the good professor bundled up warmly again, buttoning his surtout coat closely around him, and walked briskly back to his rooms. The walk was enough to produce a warm glow on his skin without inducing fatigue.

Back at his lodgings, Professor Hamilton got out of his overcoat, put some hot coals on the fire, and proceeded to take some scientific measurements and readings. He then went to the far side of the room, where he began to conduct scientific observations with regard to the atmosphere. He observed the readings on the barometer and thermometer, recording air pressure, dew point, and temperature. Next, the professor went outside to check his hygrometer and record the velocity and direction of the wind.

Professor Hamilton had been engaged in his scientific endeavors for about half an hour inside his apartment and had been standing in the cold outside for about ten minutes, recording his data, when it occurred. At first, he began to feel a pain in his left leg, as if someone were pulling one of the hairs. The pain was sharp but localized. Soon, though, the pain grew in intensity, feeling now more like the sting of a wasp or hornet, although the professor knew it was too cold for either insect to be about.

He placed his hand on the affected area, but this only

seemed to intensify the pain. Hamilton began to repeatedly pat or slap the part of his leg that was hurting—and the pain increased even more, causing him to cry out loud.

At this point, Hamilton looked down at the affected area of his left leg. To his great surprise, he saw a small flame coming from the spot. It was light in color but distinct, and its diameter at the base was about the size of a ten-cent piece. The jet of flame was somewhat convex, being flattened on top, and seemed to be the color of "quicksilver."

Knowing that the most effective way to put out a fire is to cut off its source of oxygen, Professor Hamilton cupped his hands over the growing flame, closing them together tightly to block the flow of air to it. Luckily, this action had the desired effect and the flame went out.

Once the source of his pain had been extinguished, the curious professor, while dressing his wound, carefully wrote down his observations regarding the flame's nature. What he found was most unusual. This had been no ordinary fire; no spark had ignited his clothing, for except for a slight "frosting" on the pants leg opposite the flame, the cloth was otherwise unaffected. It was Hamilton's left leg itself that had burst into flame—it had burned from the inside out, not the other way around!

Fortunately for the professor, the area of his leg burned by the flame was quite small. Had it been much larger, however, it is doubtful that Hamilton would have survived to tell the tale. His scientific knowledge of the nature of fire had been the key to his survival, and he had had the presence of mind to employ exactly the right method to extinguish the flame.

Although small, the wound caused by the flame was most severe. After applying salves for several days, Professor Hamilton went to a local physician, Dr. John Overton, for further assistance. This physician, aided by the professor's own precise observations, was able to diagnose the episode as a case of spontaneous human combustion.

He may not have realized it at the time, but Professor

Hamilton was one very lucky fellow. Spontaneous human combustion (SHC), although well documented in forensic reports since the early nineteenth century, remains a mysterious phenomenon. SHC is almost always fatal, and in almost every other known case, the victim of SHC, once he or she had burst into flame, was quickly incinerated.

Fortunately, people do not suddenly burst into flame every day of the week—but when "auto-ignition" does occur, the results can be horrific. Witnesses who have observed the beginning of a case of SHC have noted that it starts with a small jet of flame—just as it did with Professor Hamilton. But the flame usually spreads "with extreme rapidity" over a large portion of the body, burning with the intensity of a blast furnace. Within several seconds, a victim can be engulfed in flames.

SHC does not behave like ordinary fire; in fact, it violates the known laws of chemistry and physics. The flame does not radiate heat evenly; rather, it burns extremely hot within a limited space, often leaving surrounding surfaces completely untouched. In the case of a man who burst into flame in his car in 1951, when the police examined the vehicle, the damage to the car was limited to the area around the driver's seat and did not spread to the rest of the passenger compartment—yet it was so intense that it partially melted the steel dashboard! In another case, in Falkirk, Scotland, in 1904, a widow was burned to a crisp in her comfy chair—yet the cushions and pillows of the chair were not even scorched.

Professor Hamilton was lucky in another respect: the method he used to extinguish the flame. In a number of cases, persons running to the rescue of a victim have tried to douse the flames with water. When they did so, the flame flared into a raging inferno. The heat of spontaneous human combustion is so intense that water coming in contact with the fire is immediately separated into the elements of hydrogen and oxygen, each of which is highly combustible. By smothering the flame instead of trying to drown it with water, James Hamilton saved his life.

The earliest scientific accounts of human combustion first appeared in the seventeenth century—although
there are a few reports that go back all the way back to the
Dark Ages. Throughout the nineteenth century, reports of
SHC occupied quite a bit of space in the scholarly journals, and various theories, many of which seem laugh-
able today, were put forth to explain it. Leading novelists
of the day—Dickens, Balzac, Melville, and Mark Twain—
often wrote about this strange phenomenon.

It was commonly thought that self-combustion was
due to behavioral causes—alcoholism in particular.
Many of the upper-class male physicians writing on the
subject cited case studies of obese, alcoholic females of
the lower classes to prove their theories. The combina-
tion of fat, a high blood-alcohol content, and warm
woolen clothing was somehow thought to induce a person to burst into flames.

Beyond their flawed logic, such theories seemed to
be more a reflection of the researchers' class prejudices
than a serious approach to science. James Hamilton was
a case in point. According to Dr. Overton's report, the
thirty-five-year-old professor was temperate in his drinking and, if anything, probably a bit underweight—the
meager pay of an academic being the prime cause of
Hamilton's poor diet and intestinal problems.

Nowadays, scientists prefer to ignore the strange
phenomenon of SHC. For one thing, SHC violates all pre-
conceived notions regarding the laws of nature. For another, there are no lucrative government grants to
subsidize such research. For the most part, the only place
one is likely to read about spontaneous human combustion these days are in obscure coroner's reports and
sometimes dubious accounts in the tabloid press.

One modern scientist, an acquaintance of Arthur C.
Clarke, tried to explain away SHC by theorizing that the
victims' clothing acts as a sort of wick. By experimenting
with burning rolled-up clothing, the scientist tried to
show how winter clothing could contain and direct a
slow-burning fire. While that could account for how the
flame might avoid scorching the area surrounding it, in

the end, the scientist's theory is no better than those concocted by his nineteenth century predecessors, for the fire of spontaneous human combustion is anything but slow-burning. Once the jet of flame appears, the fire spreads rapidly, growing in size and intensity.

Modern science cannot even begin to explain why and how SHC starts in the first place, much less how a human body can suddenly burst into flame and generate temperatures in excess of three thousand degrees Fahrenheit. Since SHC cannot be fitted into the modern scientific dogma, science has chosen to ignore it, instead. The secrets of this strange—some would say supernatural—phenomenon remain an utter and complete mystery.

Perhaps someday someone will blow the dust off the old journals of medicine containing the accounts of Professor Hamilton's brush with death and will use it to help unravel the mystery of the "fire from heaven"—and make better sense than we of the case of the combustible professor.

TENNESSEE VALLEY APPARITIONS

28

LORETTA AND THE SPOOKS: THE HAUNTING OF HURRICANE MILLS

WITHOUT QUESTION, LORETTA LYNN IS one of the living legends of country music. Her songs have been heard and loved by millions for decades. Certainly, if anyone epitomizes the spirit of country music, it is Loretta Lynn.

Loretta's association with things of the spirit, however, extends beyond country music. For the plain truth is that the Queen of Country Music is psychic—and her antebellum home in the small town of Hurricane Mills contains more spooks than you can shake a Ouija board at!

Understandably, Loretta's encounters with the supernatural have received considerably less attention than have the other aspects of her life and career. But Loretta has never denied her psychic experiences, and whenever anyone has asked, she has been quite straightforward about discussing them.

Loretta first became aware of her unique gifts soon after marrying her childhood sweetheart, "Doo" (Oliver Doolittle Lynn Jr., also known as Mooney). She was fourteen years old, seven months pregnant, and living away from her parents for the first time in her life. Homesick, Loretta was thinking about her mom and dad quite a bit. She soon began to realize that she knew when her mother was expecting a letter from her—and more remarkably, Loretta always knew in advance when she was about to receive a letter from her mother.

Over the years, she has often had premonitions that have come true only a short while later. One night, Loretta had a terrible nightmare. In it, she dreamed that her father was dead. The dream was quite vivid—down to the color of the coffin and her father's funeral suit—and seemed so real that Loretta woke up screaming in the middle of the night, crying and shaking.

When Loretta told her husband about the nightmare, Mooney tried to reassure her, saying it was a sign that there would soon be a wedding in the family. A soon as Loretta calmed down, she tried to wipe the dream from her mind and go back to sleep.

But when Loretta went back to sleep, she had the same dream—this time more vivid and in greater detail. She saw herself walking around the coffin, crying and wringing her hands, and staring down at the face of the father laid out in his coffin.

No sooner had Loretta awakened than she received a phone call from back east. Her father had died from a massive stroke at 8 A.M., just after arriving at work that day—3 A.M. Loretta's time. She had had her first nightmare at the exact time that her father was dying.

Some years later, Loretta returned to Butcher Hollow, Kentucky, the place where she had grown up. When she visited the little mountain shack that had been her home, she saw the ghost of her father sitting on the front porch.

By 1967, Loretta Lynn had attained a large measure of success in her music career. But she and her husband were looking for a larger place for their family, someplace farther out in the country. One day, they were riding around in Humphreys County, some sixty miles west of Nashville. They had been seeking a certain place a real estate agent had told them about but had gotten lost on a back road after taking a wrong turn.

As they came over a rise, Loretta saw it—an antebellum mansion with tall white columns, looking for all the world like something out of *Gone With the Wind* as it sat high on a hill overlooking the tiny town of Hurricane Mills nestled below it. Instantly, Loretta knew this was the home for her—she had to have it. Jumping up and down in the front seat of the car, like a little girl who had just gotten a dollhouse for Christmas, Loretta told Mooney this was the house she had been dreaming of.

Her husband tried to instill a bit of reality into the discussion. They didn't know if the house was for sale, or even if they could afford it. But Loretta would hear none of it. As it turned out, not only the house but the entire little mill town was for sale!

Although buying the property would put a strain on their finances, luck—or fate—was on their side, and the couple purchased Loretta's dream house. While Loretta went on the road to perform, Mooney set about fixing up the old mansion. It was a monumental task, for the house was in terrible condition, but, bit by bit, Mooney restored the decaying dwelling and the outbuildings, and even transformed the place into a functioning ranch—all to please his child-bride.

Soon after moving in, however, Loretta and Mooney began to discover some unusual things about the house. For one thing, on several occasions when Loretta was in her room at night, she would see the door to the adjacent bedroom—the room where her twins slept—open and close all by itself.

The twins, Peggy and Patsy, were still toddlers, old enough to talk but not old enough to understand about the supernatural. Soon after settling into their new surroundings, the children began telling their mom about the "people in our room." The twins told Loretta that they often saw women dressed in long, old-fashioned dresses, with their hair "piled up high on their head." The girls were too young to even realize that the "people" were not living persons, and so were unafraid of the nighttime visitors.

They Lynns also found out that there had been a skirmish nearby during the Civil War and that nineteen Rebel soldiers were buried right on the grounds of the mansion. A few years after moving in, Loretta's eldest son, Ernest, woke up in the middle of the night to find a Confederate soldier standing at the foot of his bed. Terrified, Ernest closed his eyes tight for a very long time. When he opened them again, the ghost had vanished.

Loretta was less complacent about the antebellum apparitions. From experience, she realized that she generally had more to fear from the living than the dead, but she still vowed not to spend a minute alone in the house.

Another disquieting feature of the mansion was its "slave pit." Under the broad, cheery, sun-drenched front porch was hidden a cramped, dark cellar with heavy iron bars on the windows. It was a relic from a darker period in the building's history, from a time when slaves were imprisoned there as punishment for minor infractions against their white masters. The very idea of that foreboding and sinister place lying right beneath her family's living room gave Loretta a bad case of the willies.

In 1983, Loretta was sitting in the front parlor, watching television with a friend named Sue when they both heard footsteps on the front porch. The porch light was on, but when the women peered out the window, there was no one to be seen. The two then walked to the large recreation room in the rear of the house to see if someone might be back there, but again, no one was in evidence.

Loretta and Sue returned to the parlor and began watching television once more, but it was not long before they heard the footsteps again. This time, though, it sounded as if whoever was walking about was dragging one leg—almost as if the leg were pulling a chain and dragging it along the floorboards. The two tried to ignore the disturbances and watch the TV, but then noises began to emanate from the slave pit directly beneath where they were sitting.

On other occasions, Loretta has sat in the family room off her spacious country kitchen and felt as though something invisible were passing right by her. In the same room, there are paintings which, no matter how many times they are straightened, always seem to end up tipped to one side or another. Even the usually level-headed Mooney has heard things going up and down the stairs on occasion. Loretta later found out her husband was not telling her about these incidents for fear that she might become worried.

Eventually, Loretta resolved to hold a series of séances to try to speak to some of those who had died but whose spirits still resided in the house. During one session, the table they were sitting around moved clear across the room of its own volition. More often, though, the table moved just a bit, as a way of answering questions.

On one such occasion, Loretta and friends were trying to "raise up" a spirit, and the table spelled out that they were reaching a man named Anderson. The group tried to communicate with him further and asked a series questions. The spirit got angry at their continued probing and started shaking the table violently.

There in the dark, Loretta watched as the large hardwood table literally jumped off the floor into mid-air and then come crashing down again, collapsing right before her eyes.

The next day, Loretta inquired among the local folk in Hurricane Mills to see if anyone knew about a man named Anderson. It turned out that the original owner of the mansion was one James Anderson—and that he was buried very close to the house. Loretta never tried contacting him again.

With her cozy country home in Hurricane Mills awash in apparitions and Lord knows what else, one might imagine that Loretta would be wanting to pack up and move back to the city. Nothing could be further from the truth.

Having grown up in the hardscrabble hills of eastern Kentucky, and having made it to the very summit of the volatile music industry, it would take considerably more than a few wayward haints to intimidate the Coal Miner's Daughter. But her attraction to the house may be more than just having a permanent place to call home.

As Loretta once put it, "The place just sort of drawed

me to it." Loretta and Mooney had no notion the place even existed until that fateful Sunday in 1967 when they stumbled on Hurricane Mills. Yet, Loretta knew instantly that this house was meant for her.

"I had never heard of reincarnation," she explained, "but I felt strongly that I had lived in that house before— either that or I dreamed about it over and over."

The bond between Loretta and her home may be one which transcends both life and time, it seems. Call it coincidence, fate, or mysticism—for Loretta, it is enough just to call it home.

29

THE SPIRITS OF LYNCHBURG

IF LYNCHBURG, TENNESSEE (POPULATION 361), is about anything, it is about the good things in life. Nothing fancy, mind you—the good things never are— just good food, good drink, good company, and maybe a good story or two told around the potbellied stove. Some may call that old-fashioned, but the folks in Lynchburg don't think so—and even if it is, I'm not sure that they really care much.

Lynchburg, of course, is home to the Jack Daniel's Distillery, maker of the world's finest sippin' whiskey— bar none. It is not only the town's main industry—it is Lynchburg's *only* industry. Jack Daniel and his distillery have, over the years, become something of an institution in Tennessee—particularly in Lynchburg—and although Gentleman Jack himself has been dead and buried these many years, his spirit still presides over this place.

Most people would agree that, at least in a figurative sense, Jack Daniel still watches over the making of his spirits. But there are those who claim that the spirit of the dapper distiller, in a very literal sense, still presides over the liquor-making operation.

When the first pioneers came over the mountains, most brought with them knowledge of how to make their own private decoctions. Given the difficulty of getting their farm produce to distant markets, it seemed to many of these rugged individuals that the easiest way to prevent their cash crops from spoiling was to liquefy them. True native Tennesseans have been doing this ever since.

Of course, every distiller since the old days has thought his recipe the best and kept its formula a closely guarded secret. The Jack Daniel's formula, for example, is more closely guarded than Area 51. In a sense, though, the secret formula to Jack Daniel's sour mash whiskey is really no secret at all. Craftsmanship, quality, pride, and patience—those are the real secret ingredients to Jack Daniel's sippin' whiskey.

The founder, Gentleman Jack himself, demanded no less than the best in everything he and his distillers did. That is why, over the years, despite all the changes occurring elsewhere in the world and the decline in quality of just about everything else, Jack Daniel's whiskey remains phenomenally popular.

One "secret" that makes Jack Daniel's so smooth on the palette is the water used to produce it. In the side of one of the hills that girdle Lynchburg, and overlooking the distillery, lies a cave from which gushes forth a natural spring of pure, sweet limestone water.

Caves are wondrous things—cave springs doubly so. It was just such a place that Ponce de Leon and Desoto were searching for when they tramped about the South. Had they stopped by Lynchburg and sipped water from this source, they might have declared their respective searches at an end.

The folks in Lynchburg make no claims of eternal youth for the waters that emerge from the cave spring, but they do say some strange things have been known to happen in its vicinity.

Just outside the cave, for example, stands a large statue of Jack Daniel—austere in his long frock coat, broad-brimmed hat, and boots—looking out over the hollow that holds the distillery and town beyond. Some say the statue is more than just bronze and stone, that, somehow, the very essence of Jack Daniel still resides there, keeping a watchful eye on all that transpires below him.

To the best of my knowledge, no one has actually seen the ghost of Gentleman Jack walking the grounds of the cave or distillery, but workers from time to time have reported hearing footsteps—like the sound of old-fashioned riding boots—pacing about the distillery. To veteran ears, it sounds like someone making the rounds, checking each of the stations and every piece of equipment.

Even when no sounds can be heard, there is still the feeling of being watched—a sense that there is an invisible presence presiding over the operation there, making absolutely sure that everything is done according to the original formula. For Gentleman Jack, nothing less would be acceptable.

Down in the town of Lynchburg, another spirit abides as well. This spirit, while not as well known to outsiders, is as closely tied to the town and its traditions as is Jack Daniel.

Since 1908, Miss Mary Bobo and her boarding house, or "hotel," have been permanent fixtures in Lynchburg. Her establishment, in its heyday, was the finest hotel in town—the *only* hotel in town, in fact. In the 1970s, Miss Mary stopped taking in boarders; but her midday dinners had long been the main feature at the boarding house, and those continued nonstop until she passed away in 1983, at the age of 103.

For a time after Miss Mary's passing, it seemed as though her boarding house-style restaurant, Lynchburg's second-most venerated institution, would also pass away. But Mary Bobo's Boarding House had become so closely entwined with the distillery—for years, distillery guides had been recommending the fare at Miss Mary's to visitors—that preserving the traditions of the afternoon dinners was a natural extension of what the distillery was doing already. As a result, the distillery bought the old boarding house.

On May 1, 1984, Miss Mary Bobo's Boarding House—without boarders, of course—reopened for business. As always, dinner is served at 1 P.M. (only Yankees and cityfolk would eat their main meal of the day in the evening). Seating at Miss Mary's is "family style," with everyone sitting down at a large common table. The food is simply put on the table, you help yourself, and then pass it on.

Presiding over every aspect of dinner, just as Mary might have done, is Miss Lynne Tolley. A great-great-grand-niece of Jack Daniel and a fourth-generation Lynchburg native, Lynne Tolley is well-qualified to step into Miss Mary's shoes. Her father was the chief distiller at Jack Daniel's for many years, and she herself was working for the company when they gave her the nod to take charge of the restaurant.

Lynne had been away to college and earned a degree, but nobody held that against her. She was from a good family and, more to the point, knew how to cook up a storm.

Miss Mary operated the restaurant for so many years that it was only natural that she should have left her mark on the place. In fact, the whole house seems to be imbued with the aura of her personality. But when Lynne began to work at Mary Bobo's, she began to sense that perhaps Miss Mary was not so departed as the dear departed ought to be.

Miss Mary was always a good housekeeper—meticulous, in fact. If something were taken out, it was put back where it belonged; if a piece of bric-a-brac was moved, it would be set back exactly where she had had it. Chairs and tables were all arranged just so by Miss Mary. That's just the way she always did things—and that's just the way she still does things.

When I talked with Lynne Tolley down in Lynchburg, she didn't know much about Gentleman Jack haunting his distillery, but she was quite certain that Miss Mary Bobo continues to linger in the renovated hostelry. Miss Mary is not a scary ghost, by any means, but to those familiar with the house, her presence is unmistakable. Working there day in and day out, Lynne and her staff often notice that doors left open even a brief time will close all by themselves within a few minutes.

Objects left in plain sight have often been known to disappear. A thorough search will be made, to no avail, but then the missing object will turn up all by itself.

Lynne has noticed that just about any item in the restaurant that has been left out by visitors will be back in its appropriate place the next time she looks—be it the lid on a mint jar or a chair pulled out from a table. Lynne's staff is good—but not that good!

As with Gentleman Jack, there are no moans or groans, no chains or other rude noises. But Miss Mary Bobo haunts her boarding house restaurant nonetheless. There is nothing to fear, though, for in life, Miss Mary was a good soul, and her spirit has remained benevolent since returning to her favorite haunts.

I would be remiss if I didn't at least mention yet another denizen of Lynchburg. It's not a phantom, exactly, although it can be as elusive as one. The locals call it the Wyooter, and a number of stories and legends are told about it in Lynchburg.

The Wyooter, as near as can be discerned, is a four-legged beast, but of what genus or species, known or unknown, is a matter of some speculation. The very few who have seen it have never returned to tell the tale. My personal opinion is that the Wyooter is related to the Wampus Cat, a weird beast in East Tennessee known to frequent moonshine stills.

The late photographer Joe Clark, whose evocative pictures of Lynchburg graced magazine ads for Jack Daniel's whiskey for many years, was one of the first to encounter the legendary beast. Since then, others have met with various degrees of success in trying to catch a glimpse of it.

The Wyooter is reputed to dwell in the same cave from which flows the springwater used to make Jack Daniel's. Visitors to the nearby monument to Gentleman Jack have on occasion reported hearing a low growling sound coming from the cave.

Since Joe Clark's passing, resident folklorist and all-around good ol' boy Roger Brashears has been the leading expert on the haunts and habits of the Wyooter. Listening to Roger talk, however, the Wyooter begins to sound as if it might be able to give Paul Bunyan a run for his money.

By Roger's account, the Wyooter is more powerful than an eighteen-wheeler and is as big as a barn. In fact, the Wyooter is so big and strong that the only way to escape from the creature is to run through its legs, since it is too large to be able to turn around quickly. It has never been known to harm a Lynchburg native, although it has scared quite a few. Perhaps it is the magic of that elixir they make in Lynchburg which has a calming effect on the beast.

Stories of encounters with the Wyooter abound and would fill several books if all were told. Talking with Roger, it is at times difficult to tell where the facts leave off and the legend begins. For the unbelievers among us, Mr. Brashears is able to provide proof positive of the Wyooter's existence: a photo taken by renowned photographer Joe Clark of an albino Wyooter.

Like Bigfoot, no Wyooter has ever been captured alive—but it is not for lack of trying. Last Halloween, folks in Lynchburg organized a Wyooter hunt in an effort to track down the beast. The creature was a no show—it wasn't cold enough for him, claims Roger Brashears.

On leaving the hollow in which Lynchburg nestles, it almost seems as if the whole village will fade into the mist behind you—it has that effect on people. But Roger Brashears would probably say there is more Lorna Doone about the place than *Brigadoon*. Regardless, there is no doubt, in my mind at least, that there is something unusual going on in Lynchburg. The town has a special enchantment all its own that is due in no small part to the spirit of its inhabitants—living and dead.

30

CIGARS FROM MARS?
STRANGE VISITORS OVER
THE VALLEY

NOWADAYS, THE BELIEF IN UNIDENTIFIED flying objects—UFOs—has become almost commonplace. From serious encounters to *E. T.* lollipops, whatever their basis in fact, the idea of spacecraft visiting earth is no longer such an alien concept.

It is commonly assumed that sightings of such craft—whatever the truth of the matter may be—are a phenomenon spawned by the Atomic Age, a by-product of our technological mastery of space and energy. It comes as something of a surprise, therefore, to discover that the Mid-South may have played host to unearthly visitors nearly a century ago, before most people could even entertain the notion of space travel. While not exactly in the realm of the supernatural, it is, at the very least, quite strange.

In the early years of the twentieth century, the Tennessee Valley was a far different place than it is now. Today, cities such as Huntsville, Knoxville, and Chattanooga boast of booming industries and modern research facilities, many of which are on the cutting edge of space technology. In the early years of this century, however, it was a far different story.

The Tennessee Valley, like much of the South, was

still rural and in many ways was still trying to recover from the effects of the Civil War. Folks in the countryside lacked many basic amenities, while people in the cities were not much better off. In the Mid-South, not only were airships and airplanes a rarity, they were virtually nonexistent.

In general, aerial flight had only just emerged from the realm of science fiction into science fact. By the beginning of 1910, in all the United States there were but four lighter-than-air craft known to exist, and none of them were in the South.

It came as some surprise, therefore, when on January 13, 1910, a large object of unknown origin suddenly appeared over the city of Chattanooga.

It was Wednesday morning, about eleven o'clock, and the staff in the editorial offices of the *Chattanooga News* was wrestling with the usual news items—murder, floods, racial unrest, local politics, river traffic, and the like—when the phone rang. A reporter received a call from a somewhat excited gentleman with urgent news. He had called to inform the paper of the arrival of a large "airship" in the skies above the city. The caller, noticeably agitated by what he had seen, said the object had appeared on the south side of town, was heading northward, and should be visible over Terminal Station by now.

By the time the newsman had hung up and the staffers could open a window and crane their necks about, the "airship" was already overhead—passing a little east of the newspaper's offices and almost directly over the Albert Theater.

When first sighted by the reporters and editors, the craft was cruising at close to a thousand feet and moving very rapidly. It was self-propelled, the newspaper later observed, since at that time there was no breeze—the flags were hanging limp on their poles, and smoke from the stacks of the factories in town was "low and lifeless." That eliminated the possibility of the craft being some stray hot-air balloon.

While observers at first thought the object might be

an airplane of some sort, as it came closer and they could see its cigar-shaped profile, it seemed to more closely resemble a "dirigible balloon" or airship. The cigar-shaped craft was light in color—white or a bright silver—and some witnesses thought they even saw a "navigator" piloting it from underneath. The eyewitness reporter for the News was more cautious, writing simply that "a black object below the stays much resembled a man."

In any case, the vessel, having appeared over the south part of town, made rapid progress across the downtown district, passing over Terminal Station, the Albert Theater and then proceeding northward, passing west of the new Presbyterian Church and east of Centenary, finally disappearing into a mysterious thick cloud that was hanging over the river north of town.

The event—which caused no small amount of curiosity and consternation—lasted all of ten minutes. The vessel, whatever it was, appeared to be traveling at a rapid rate. Attempts to locate the mystery ship over the towns just north of Chattanooga proved fruitless. The cigar-shaped craft had vanished without a trace.

As reports of sighting came in to the newsroom throughout the day, it became clear that Chattanooga was not the only city to be favored with its appearance. The day before, it seems, Huntsville, Alabama, had also had a visitation.

An "airship" of similar color and size to the craft sighted over Chattanooga had appeared over Huntsville late on the afternoon of January 12. The craft was sighted around 4:30 in the afternoon, coming from out of the southwest and headed in a straight line toward the northeast, following the contour of the Tennessee Valley.

The Huntsville craft was traveling at a great height, so it was difficult for eyewitnesses to tell whether it was "an aeroplane, an airship, or a dirigible balloon." The craft was moving so fast that by the time people could get hold of a pair of binoculars to get a closer look, it was gone. Some idea of the craft's velocity can be gleaned from one report, which stated that "the speed appeared to be greater than any wind short of a hurricane."

The object was last seen in East Huntsville, where it disappeared behind the mountains—apparently on a course toward Chattanooga.

The mystery airship quickly became a source of "great wonderment" and not a little speculation. Hundreds had witnessed its passage across Chattanooga on Thursday, and throughout the remainder of the day and on into the next morning there was much discussion—not all of it serious—in the barbershops and drinking establishments around town.

Some professed to have seen a man, suspended by wires, piloting the craft. One man was heard to remark that perhaps it was a local merchant, "hunting for the Chamber of Commerce, where he wished to make a donation." Another wit ventured the opinion that a certain politician who was known to be on shaky ground with his constituency was piloting the airship and had taken to the skies to discover "where it is at."

The wits and wisecrackers went slack-jawed around eleven, however, when the "peculiar aircraft" again appeared over the city. This time, however, the mystery ship was headed in a southeasterly direction—on a heading toward the city of Atlanta. On this day, however, the sky was very cloudy, and so it was very difficult to get more than a glimpse of the craft.

The local papers and government authorities were flooded with hundreds of calls from people inquiring where the craft had come from. Meanwhile, scores of folks in the streets "rubbernecked" to catch sight of it overhead. The rubberneckers were no wiser for all their efforts, for the strange craft soon disappeared to the southeast, crossing over Missionary Ridge and leaving as it came—in a cloud of mystery.

This was not the end of it, however. Late on January 14, a craft of similar design also appeared over Knoxville. It was just before 7 P.M. and the sky was already dark when the mysterious object was sighted over the city. Several citizens swore they observed it overhead in the darkening winter sky, and two men who were on Summit Hill at the time claimed its outlines were fairly distinct.

"Sparks"—lights of some sort—were said to be visible on the craft, and many who observed its passage assumed the sparkling lights were coming from the engines propelling it.

Again, to the eyes of those who witnessed it, it appeared to be a "dirigible balloon," that is, it was cigar-shaped in design. When last seen that night, the craft was heading in a southerly direction.

What is one to make of this high strangeness? Was the mystery airship merely the antics of some stray balloonatic—just so much hot air?

At first glance, the strange craft sighted over the cities of the Tennessee Valley in January 1910 appeared to be of terrestrial origin. After all, a number of people said they saw a pilot and described the craft as a dirigible or airship.

But there is a natural tendency among humans to try to fit everything we see into a known category; we do this unconsciously every day of our lives. When confronted with an event or object that does conform to a familiar pattern or form, the mind will still try to force it into one. It is an easy matter, therefore, to assume that an unusual object in the sky is some sort of lighter-than-air vessel, and that the dark object beneath it is a pilot.

The fact is that at the beginning of 1910, there were just four lighter-than-air vessels in the United States. Jane's *All the World's Airships* for 1909 listed all manner of lighter-than-air craft, and while many were on drawing boards, most of them were little more than a gleam in an inventor's eye. Of the four such craft in the United States that were known to be capable of flight, none could manage a speed of more than twenty-five miles per hour, and none were anywhere near the Tennessee Valley in January 1910.

Even assuming that some enterprising inventor had put together an airship and been able to cruise south unseen, neither the four existing craft nor any that had been proposed were capable of anything approaching the speed of the craft the eyewitnesses described. During each of the four sightings, the mystery airship was described as traveling at a high rate of speed—even in dead air. Such speeds were beyond even the capability of airplanes of the day.

There is no question of the airship being any sort of hoax; it was seen by too many people in broad daylight. Nor was it the invention of some bored editor on a slow news day—not with the whole city as eyewitnesses. Nor was it any aircraft known to exist at the time. One cannot help but conclude that this object—whatever it was and wherever it came from—was not of this earth.

In New England, less than a month before the sightings in the South, residents of Boston and surrounding towns had observed similar craft. Those reports, too, indicated a craft with abilities far beyond the technology of the time. Of course, in both the New England and Tennessee Valley sightings, what could not be explained away was quickly ignored by the men of science and politics.

Still, an objective look at the facts forces one to conclude that then, as now, the words of the *Chattanooga News* reporter ring true: "We are being spied upon."

31

THE SHADES OF SHILOH

WHAT I SAW AT SHILOH: VERDANT FIELDS and placid groves of fruit and shade trees, and a white-washed wooden church christened with the Hebrew name for "peace." A most unlikely place to find hell.

To this day, the very name "Shiloh" brings to mind images of death, destruction, and the horrors of war. With such untold human suffering as once occurred here, is it any wonder that visitors and area residents have reported restless spirits haunting the killing fields of Shiloh?

One would not have thought such horror possible before that fateful April morning in 1862. General Ulysses S. Grant's Army of the Tennessee was encamped near the banks of the Tennessee River, awaiting the arrival of another army under the command of General Don Carlos Buell. On the border of Tennessee and Mississippi, the rolling meadows that stretched from Shiloh Church to Pittsburg Landing were dotted with tents—the site had been selected by Grant's second in command, William T. Sherman, as the staging area for their invasion of the Deep South.

Though poised to invade the heartland of the Confederacy, Sherman, strangely, had taken no precautions to defend the camp against a surprise attack. Grant was not even with his army; he was miles away, in Savannah, Tennessee, lolling in the luxury of Cherry Mansion, his headquarters.

At daybreak on April 6, the Union camp was just beginning to stir. Many soldiers were still dozing in their tents, while a few were up and busy, huddled around campfires making breakfast. The gray morning mist still hung low in the hollows and between the trees.

Suddenly, from out of the mist came hordes of gray-clad men, charging straight for the tents with bayonets fixed and screaming like banshees. The Confederates were among the campsites before anyone knew what was happening, bayoneting men as they slept and shooting down Bluebellies like so many hogs. It was not so much a battlefield as a slaughterhouse.

Quickly overrunning the Union encampment, the Confederates might have wiped out the fleeing Federal army right there and then, had the starving Rebels not stopped to eat the breakfasts still simmering on the cookfires.

Sherman, only lately recovered from a nervous breakdown, was still in something of a fog. At first, he could not grasp what was happening—not till an orderly was shot down right next to him.

Stunned and confused, the Yankee survivors tried to make a fighting withdrawal toward the riverboat landing. But with officers dead or separated from their men, and units mixed altogether, the situation was hopelessly confused.

Where was Grant during all this? The general, it seems, was having a leisurely breakfast at Cherry Mansion, some ten miles to the north. Army gossip at the time had it that Grant was badly hungover—he and his staff had been drinking heavily the night before—and was possibly still drunk when he finally arrived at the battle. That, according to gossip, was the reason Grant was so confused and disoriented on the morning of the battle. Although Grant later claimed to have arrived at Shiloh by eight o'clock, eyewitnesses place his arrival on the scene closer to 10 A.M.

In any case, it was already too late for Grant to avert disaster. The Union army would likely have been driven into the river by the Rebs had not Generals Lew Wallace and Benjamin Prentiss managed to rally the retreating

Federal troops and make a last-ditch stand in a sunken road that stretched across the battlefield. Here, they fought a desperate fight, repulsing repeated Confederate assaults. The Rebels referred to the site as "the Hornet's Nest." Grant sent no reinforcements to aid Wallace and Prentiss, and when the southerners brought up their field artillery, they blew the defenders to pieces, but the Yankees' heroic stand had saved their army.

That night, in a cold and driving rain, the wounded of both sides lay exposed to the elements and suffering. Half-wild hogs roamed the fields, gnawing on the dead and dying. Had not Buell's Army of the Ohio arrived on the scene late that night, there is good reason to believe that Grant's survivors would have been wiped out the following morning.

As it was, the combined Union armies mounted an offensive the next day and retook the ground lost in the previous fracas. Commanders on both sides claimed victory; which general was the bigger liar remains a matter of conjecture.

Since that time, those who have visited the site where the two armies clashed have on occasion reported hearing a ghostly gun battle on those fatal fields. Musketfire and the screams of wounded men have been heard. There seems to be little or no regularity to such encounters, although some people have claimed to hear these sounds on the anniversary of the battle.

If one were to pinpoint the spot most frequently cited as the source of such activities, the Hornet's Nest would probably seem the most favored. Here was where the Yankees made their last stand, and here was where General Wallace was wounded and left for dead, lying unprotected all night as the cold, cold rain came down.

The Federal bureaucrats who run the military park deny any and all supernatural occurrences at Shiloh. The official line is that there is no basis for the belief that the Shiloh battlefield is haunted—and there is no record of any stories about ghosts at Shiloh.

That is the official line, but the fact that visitors are not allowed in the park after sunset, the very time when the shades of dead soldiers would be most likely to roam, hinders any attempt to refute the government's story. But residents who live near the park, and on a part of the battlefield, often have a different story to tell.

Shiloh Estates is a modern subdivision adjacent to the national military park. At least two civil war ghosts have been reported haunting that part of the battlefield, and perhaps there are many more. One resident, a professor at nearby Freed Hardeman University, claims that when the moon is full and the night air clear, he can hear General Braxton Bragg and his Confederates out there, talking and fighting.

In addition to ghostly gun battles, there is also the legend of the Drummer Boy of Shiloh. According to the story, on the second day of battle, a drummer boy with a regiment in Buell's army was ordered to sound "attack" on his drum. Responding to the drummer's call, the regiment moved forward, storming a Confederate position on a hilltop. The union troops met stiff resistance and their attack stalled halfway up the hill.

The commanding officer ordered the drummer boy to beat "retreat." The youngster began to play, but once again he sounded "attack."

"I said beat 'retreat,' " bellowed the officer. "But sir," said the lad, " 'attack' is all I know. I never learned 're-treat'!"

By now it was too late, for the regiment had moved to attack. To everyone's surprise, the attack carried the day as the Rebel strongpoint fell, turning the tide of battle. When the officer looked for the drummer boy, to commend him for his valor, he found the lad lying on the hillside with his drum still at his side—and a bullet through his heart.

Since that day, it is said, if one stands on that particular slope at a certain time of day, one may still faintly hear the rat-tat-tat of the heroic youngster calling the Union troops to "attack." Some even claim to have seen the Drummer Boy of Shiloh on that hill, beating out a rhythm on his drum.

Here too, officials have denied the story—just a fairy tale, they say, nothing more. But unknown to present park officials is the testimony of Captain Rice. During the 1930s and into the 1940s, Captain Rice oversaw much of the modern improvements made to the park. He also acted as unofficial historian of the park and was a leader in the movement for its preservation.

One day, Captain Rice's men were excavating a hillside in the park for a new road. In the course of their work, they stumbled on the skeleton of a young boy. Like so many of the dead at Shiloh, his body had remained where it had fallen, and had been overlooked by the burial details. The skeleton still wore pieces of a drum cord around its neck, and there was a bullet hole through its chest.

Every legend, they say, has its basis in fact. And if the story of the Drummer Boy is true—why not also the stories of encounters with his ghost?

In nearby Savannah, Cherry Mansion, which served as a Union headquarters both before and after the battle of Shiloh, has its own shades as well. No fewer than ten Federal generals stayed there during 1862, and tragedy befell several of them.

Built in 1830, the mansion boasts eighteen-inch-thick brick walls and handmade native pine interior trim. Although a slave owner, the master of the house, C. H. Cherry, was a staunch Unionist and put his mansion at the disposal of the Federal commanders.

Among the commanders who stayed at Cherry Mansion, General C. F. Smith died from a foot infection while there, and General Wallace—the hero of the Hornet's Nest—was carried to the house from the battlefield with a bullet still lodged in his brain. He lay at Cherry Mansion for three days, his wife at his side the entire time.

Besides the commanders, hundreds more casualties were brought to Savannah after the battle, and many died of their wounds there. There is no shortage of ghosts in Savannah.

For many years, the Guinn family, which owns

Cherry Mansion, has experienced strange doings in the old house. One servant reported hearing the sound of heavy footsteps running across the front porch. There seems an urgency to the pace of the steps—as if someone is carrying an important message—yet when the door is opened, there is no one to be seen!

In another instance, neighbors who were asked to keep an eye on the mansion in the owner's absence observed a man clad in what seemed to be a dark-blue uniform peering intently out the attic window as if looking for someone. It has been suggested that this recurring ghost is the shade of General Wallace, who lay abed in the house for three days before finally dying of his wounds. Whether this is so may be is impossible to determine for certain, but there is little doubt that a ghostly man in blue dwells in the historic house on Main Street.

Historians still debate Grant's mysterious behavior on the day of battle, but as we've seen, the mysteries of Shiloh and Savannah go far beyond the actions of one man. Phantom armies, strange sounds of drumming, and a mystery man in blue—these are but a few of the uncanny events and entities that still haunt the killing fields of Shiloh.

32

THE HAUNTED HOTEL
OF WARTRACE

NESTLED IN THE HEART OF TENNESSEE walking horse country lies the small community of Wartrace. Horse lovers by the thousands have come to this little railroad town over the years, and the reason for their pilgrimage can be summed up in just two words: Strolling Jim.

Strolling Jim's claim to fame lies in the fact that he was the first horse to win the laurels of World Champion Walking Horse. Some say he was not only the first but the best, as well.

Over the past several decades, the Tennessee walking horse has become a nationally renowned breed of horse. Owners, breeders, and trainers spend small fortunes (and large) to turn their mounts into another Strolling Jim. The craze began in the latter part of the nineteenth century, when gambling on horse racing was outlawed in Tennessee.

Some horse breeders moved to Kentucky, where the atmosphere was more congenial to their way of life. Others resolved that, if they couldn't race their horses, then, by gosh, they would *walk* 'em!

Spending his early years as a hard-driven plowhorse, Jim was overworked and underfed—the two-year-old gelding looked like anything but a champion. But two equine enthusiasts, Henry Davis and Floyd

Carothers, had heard that the horse had an unusual gait. Being good judges of horse flesh, they bought the animal for a nominal sum.

On their way back home, the partners noticed how the horse seemed to "stroll along"—and that is how he got the name Strolling Jim. Carothers was the proprietor of a small hotel in Wartrace named the Walking Horse Hotel, behind which he maintained the old stables in good condition. It was here that Jim was boarded.

Floyd was a skilled horse trainer, but he soon found that Strolling Jim didn't need much training—he was what they call a "natural." Soon the horse was winning first prize at walking horse competitions throughout the Mid- South. Strolling Jim's meteoric rise culminated in the World Championship, presented at the first National Walking Horse Celebration in Shelbyville, Tennessee, in 1939.

In the stables behind the hotel, Strolling Jim was treated like royalty, and in a sense he was. Jim even had his own mascot, a large black watchdog. After winning the championship, Jim continued to compete, garnering a number of blue ribbons. Eventually, Strolling Jim was sold for a record price and went on to win more awards. When Floyd Carothers died in 1944, his wife, Olive, continued to run the Walking Horse Hotel.

In 1947, Strolling Jim was at last retired from competition, and his owner at that time gave the gelding back to Mrs. Carothers. Strolling Jim spent his golden years grazing in a field behind the hotel, and when he died in 1957, Olive buried him behind the hotel.

Over the years, the hotel has become a shrine of sorts to the legendary Strolling Jim and his trainer, Floyd Carothers. Horse enthusiasts from all over the United States—even the world—come to pay homage and visit the grave of the horse that started it all.

By 1947, when Strolling Jim was retired, the watchdog was no longer around to guard the aging champion. But, by all accounts, a better protector looked over him from then on: the ghost of Floyd Carothers.

It seems that Floyd, who was also buried near the

hotel, never really left. Numerous incidents of a supernatural nature that have occurred in and around the hotel
generally have been attributed to Floyd's still-animated
spirit.

On a number of occasions, for example, guests staying at the hotel have seen the figure of a man silhouetted
against the windows of the second-floor hallway. The
window is right outside the room that Floyd occupied
when he lived there. Several local residents who knew
him in life have also claimed to have seen Carothers
prowling the upstairs hallway.

Between 1980 and 1993, the hotel was operated by
George Wright, himself an ardent walking horse enthusi-
ast. The hotel was already something of a shrine among
horsemen, and Wright renovated the structure and restored its original name—the Hotel Overall—and added
his own extensive collection of walking horse photos and
memorabilia to the displays on its walls.

Wright attributed a number of minor poltergeist-like
incidents that have occurred around the hotel to Floyd's
ghostly presence. A favorite trick of Floyd's was to play
havoc with the hotel's security cameras.

One evening in July 1991 stood out vividly in
Wright's memory. George had been very busy that night
with guests, the restaurant, and whatnot, but the ghost of
Floyd Carothers was also very busy, mercilessly bedevil-
ing the besieged innkeeper almost nonstop.

Finally, something made Wright follow a compelling
urge, or hunch, to go out behind the hotel to the stables—
if only to get away from Floyd's pesky antics. When
George arrived, he found his favorite mare about to foal.
She was having a difficult time giving birth and was in
critical need of medical help. Had George not been driven out of the hotel when he was, it is likely that both
mare and foal would have been lost. George credits the
phantom of fellow horse lover Floyd with intervening to
save the lives of his horses.

As part of the upgrade of the old hotel, Wright hired
a professional photographer to take still pictures for a
promotional brochure touting the Hotel Overall and its

restaurant. When the shots of the dining room were developed, they revealed that, in addition to table and chairs, the photographer had caught on film the presence of several bona fide ghosts as well.

Standing behind the dining room chairs in the photos were the gray gossamer forms of four ghosts. Did Floyd's phantom have a spectral reunion? Or are there still other spirits that dwell at the hotel in Wartrace?

Olive Carothers had been living in Shelbyville for a few years when she died in 1991. After her passing, many people noticed a distinct waning in Floyd's presence at the hotel. As the current owner, Bea Garland, told me, "Mr. Carothers has not been in evidence lately."

Perhaps Floyd was simply hanging around all those years waiting for Olive to join him on the other side. At any rate, according to the present proprietors, they have noticed no spectral presence about the place of late.

After a hiatus of several years, John and Bea Garland purchased the inn in 1995 and undertook a major overhaul of the Overall, changing its name back to the Walking Horse Hotel. The guest rooms have been modernized, the dining facilities improved, and a series of gift shops added on the second floor.

While the Garlands themselves have not seen or heard anything unusual, just a few years back, one group that rented the place for a night did. Some folks from the area rented the hotel for a New Year's Eve celebration, which by all accounts, was alcohol- and drug-free. Soon after midnight—the witching hour—however, there was a late arrival to the party.

The uninvited guest, they claim, was none other than Strolling Jim. The long-dead champion had risen from his resting place behind the hotel and commenced to prance about the grounds in the high-stepping gait that had made him so famous.

So, if you're traveling down Interstate 24, whether to take in the Celebration in Shelbyville or just on your way south, be sure to stop in Wartrace and pay your respects to Strolling Jim—he just might come out to greet you.

33

THE PHANTOM GOWNSMAN
OF SEWANEE

TRAVELING SOUTHWARD TOWARD CHAT-
tanooga, one invariably encounters Monteagle Mountain,
rising dramatically from the lowlands and looming omi-
nously before the eyes. The locals call it Mystery Mountain, because strange things have been known to happen
on its slopes.

Of all the uncanny things that have been reported on
Monteagle Mountain's heights, surely the strangest is that
of the Phantom Gownsman.

While several small communities crown the summit
of the mysterious mount, the most notable is Sewanee,
home to the illustrious University of the South. Sewanee
is one of the leading academic institutions in what has
sometimes been referred to as the South's "Kudzu
League."

Founded by a Confederate general who was also an
Episcopal bishop, Sewanee is steeped in southern traditions. There is much of the atmosphere of the great English universities about the campus as well. For one thing,
the faculty and many of the undergraduates are entitled
to wear the cap and gown of academia as part of their
daily garb.

All upperclassmen are inducted into the Order of the
Gownsmen, and even freshman seminary students are allowed to wear the black gown. The fact that Sewanee's

resident ghost also wears this attire has led people to think that he was perhaps a member of the student body in life.

The more credible version of the phantom's origin has it that an upperclassman was driving his car one night along the area's steep and winding mountain roads. As he rounded a sharp curve, he lost control of the vehicle and was killed, his body being horribly mangled in the wreck. The young man had been a promising student, and his untimely death was considered a tragedy.

His academic life cut short, the young scholar's spirit returned to the place that had been so congenial to him in life. Still dressed in the school's traditional gown, he roams the campus, visiting his favorite haunts. According to some versions of the tale, the fatal accident also separated the Gownsman's head from his body, and in death the two parts have not been quite able to meet up with one another.

In so serious an academic environment as Sewanee, talk of ghosts and such, while tolerated, is not given any official sanction, so very little regarding his visitations has been put to paper. The Gownsman's comings and goings have for the most part been transmitted to succeeding generations of young scholars via oral tradition. Needless to say, in some cases, the accounts have grown with the telling.

The school's seminary students, for example, often claim the phantom as one of their own and offer another explanation as to how he lost his head.

Over the years, Sewanee's seminary has produced more than eighty Episcopal bishops, and its theological curriculum can be quite rigorous. According to this version of the Gownsman tale, several years ago a number of seminary students were studying late into the night, cramming for their final examinations. One of their number wished to keep studying, while the others, worn out, wished to quit for the night.

An argument ensued, during which the lamp was knocked over and the room was plunged into darkness. When the lamp was relighted, the other students were shocked to find the young scholar's head rolling around on the floor. The budding divine's head was so crammed with learning that it had fallen off from the sheer weight of the knowledge!

Arthur Ben Chitty, one of the university's eminent alumni and unofficial keeper of the flame of its traditions, has taken note of some of the lore of gore regarding the school's headless resident. As near as he could discern from the older alumni, the Headless Gownsman (HG for short) was first observed many years ago, perhaps as far back as the 1880s, in Breslin Tower.

At that time, only a long bell rope descending from the top of the tower connected the ground to the place where the campus clock and chimneys had been installed. It was from this tower that the Headless Gownsman was originally seen to come and go. Later, when Breslin Tower was renovated and additional stories were built atop the structure, the Gownsman took to haunting Hodgson Chapel Tower—perhaps to be closer to the seminary students.

Hardly a semester goes by without a sighting of the Phantom Gownsman on the Sewanee campus. And students are not the only ones to have seen him.

One of the more reliable reports of an encounter with the Gownsman involves a former school administrator. Several years ago, Mrs. Tucker was returning home late one night from Forensic Hall. As she walked toward her car, she encountered what she at first thought to be a student, since he appeared to be wearing the academic gown that is so commonplace on campus.

The figure kept coming closer and closer, but no greeting issued from his lips. Mrs. Tucker thought that odd, since Sewanee is a relatively small campus, and students and faculty generally are familiar with one another. The figure also made no move to get out of her way—very untypical of the normally well-mannered Sewanee student.

Mrs. Tucker thought she discerned a face but could not recognize it. Then, as the shape brushed past her, as if she weren't there, she turned around to see where he was going—but the gowned figure was no longer there. There was no hiding place he could have ducked into so quickly; he had simply vanished into thin air.

The places where the phantom is most frequently sighted seem to be related in one way or another to the seminary. That is one reason some think he was once a theology student.

One odd campus tale has it that the Gownsman's head haunts the interior of the seminary students' dormitory. Years ago, the creepy cranium was reported to be haunting Wyndcliff Hall when that was the seminarian dorm, but more recently the floating head has been sighted in Saint Luke's Hall.

During times of stress, the floating head seems most in evidence in the new seminary dorm. Budding divines claim to have seen the ghost in their rooms; others swear they have heard it bouncing down the stairs—bump, bump, bump—a thump for each step in the stairwell.

The rest of the Headless Gownsman, meanwhile, is commonly sighted in silhouette, walking along the crenelated rooftops of the college buildings that huddle around the quadrangle. There are even photos that are purported to have captured the phantom on film.

While some of these reports may be dismissed as typical college pranks or tall stories, many of the accounts have the ring of authenticity about them. There are, for example, reports of inexplicable sounds heard by students and faculty at odd hours. Even those who scoff at the notion of a ghost roaming the campus have to concede that, "some very weird noises come down those hallowed halls very early in the morning."

Beyond the confines of the campus, there are other mysteries atop Monteagle Mountain—such as Bucket of Blood Cave and even occasional reports of Bigfoot roaming its slopes—but the university's Phantom Gownsman remains the most famous. Headless or not, beyond all the lore that has accumulated about him over the years lies a genuine psychic phenomenon that has yet to be fully understood.

34

THE GREEN GHOUL
OF CHICKAMAUGA

THE BATTLE OF CHICKAMAUGA WAS ONE
of the bloodiest engagements of the Civil War, second in
slaughter only to Gettysburg. Over the years, visitors to
Chickamauga, like those at Gettysburg, from time to time
have come away from the field of battle with tales of
strange and supernatural encounters.

Foremost among the reports of uncanny experiences
on the site of the bloody conflict in northern Georgia are
those related to an entity sometimes referred to as Old
Green Eyes. What it is, and how it came to haunt these
fields, is one of the unsolved mysteries of one of history's
most famous battles.

In the period leading up to Chickamauga, Confederate armies had caught Union forces off guard twice, at
Shiloh and Stones River, and had inflicted a severe maul-
ing each time. Had it not been for the Rebel commanders'
unerring knack for turning victory into defeat, at least
two Federal armies might have been wiped out.

As it was, during the summer of 1863, General
William Rosecrans, commander of the veteran Army of
the Cumberland, through a series of feints and counter-
marches, had bumfuzzled Confederate General Braxton
Bragg (not a hard thing to do) and outflanked Bragg's Army
of Tennessee, forcing it to fall back into northern Georgia.
As a result, the city of Chattanooga fell into the lap of the

Union army with hardly a shot fired. Chattanooga was the gateway to the Deep South, a strategically important city where rail, road, and river routes all intersected. A Union army occupying Chattanooga was like a sword pointed at the bowels of the Confederacy, and Rosecrans was the general chosen to do the disemboweling.

Capturing Chattanooga was one thing, but holding it was quite another. Bragg's Army of Tennessee was hurriedly reinforced with a corps from Robert E. Lee's army in Virginia, headed by the legendary commander General James Longstreet. For once, the Confederates actually had a numerical superiority over the army they meant to attack.

Rosecrans was not entirely ignorant of the situation. He knew the Rebels were planning an offensive to retake the city, and to forestall that, Rosecrans led his troops out to meet the enemy in the field. Marching through the strategic pass of McFarland's Gap, the Yankees probed the fields of northern Georgia, seeking the enemy. They found the Rebs—hordes of them.

Starting as a cavalry skirmish for possession of a bridge over a creek on September 18, the fighting quickly escalated into a full-blown scrap, with Bragg's sixty-six thousand boys in butternut and gray pitted against Rosecrans's fifty-eight thousand bluecoats. The battle raged through tangled forests and open fields on a scale unmatched previously during the war. Although sorely pressed, the Yankees pretty much held their own for two days.

As fate would have it, on the third day of battle, a Union messenger was passing close behind the line of battle, carrying a dispatch to headquarters. As he looked toward the front, he noticed what he thought was a large hole in the Federal battle line and told General Rosecrans about it. Alarmed at the potential danger, Rosecrans pulled a division out of the line to plug the supposed gap. But the gap was an imaginary one—the unit defending the position had taken cover in a nearby wood to avoid sniper and artillery fire. By shifting a division out of the line, however, Rosecrans had opened up a real gap.

By some strange twist of fate, it was at this precise moment and at this precise point in the Union line that

Longstreet chose to mount his attack. Three Confederate divisions, yelling loudly enough to shake down the mountains, came charging full tilt through the gaping hole in the Union line. With nothing to stop them, Longstreet's troops quickly overran two northern divisions and chewed up two more before Rosecrans and his staff knew what was happening.

The whole right wing of the Union army collapsed like a house of cards. Infantrymen threw down their muskets and fled, while artillerists abandoned their cannons and caissons, jumped on their horses, and galloped away. As retreat turned into rout, Rosecrans ordered his staff to flee for their lives and try to make it to Chattanooga to organize the city's defense.

By all the rules of war, the Army of the Cumberland ought to have been destroyed that afternoon. That it was not is mainly due to one man: Major General George Thomas, the Yankee from Virginia, who would that day earn the sobriquet "Rock of Chickamauga."

Commanding a division on the Union left, Thomas's command had been unaffected by the debacle on the right. But that changed around one o'clock that afternoon when Longstreet turned to deal with him. Thomas ought to have fallen back to Chattanooga and escaped while he could; instead, he ordered his men to dig in on Snodgrass Hill, the last defensible position between the enemy and the Union escape route through McFarland Gap.

Division after division of Longstreet's corps charged Thomas's position, only to be repulsed. As the afternoon wore on, the full brunt of Bragg's large army fell on that isolated command. Wave after wave of Rebels hurled themselves against the Union hedgehog on Snodgrass Hill like tidal waves, only be dashed against the Rock of Chickamauga. With nightfall, Thomas's command withdrew in good order, undefeated, and joined the rest of the army in Chattanooga.

Given the untold suffering and misery that occurred at Chickamauga, it should come as no surprise that there are a number of reports of restless spirits roaming the scene of their agonizing deaths.

The most unusual of these reports concerns a creature of uncertain origin but horrific nature, Old Green Eyes. According to legend, after the fighting had ceased on Snodgrass Hill, a strange creature with glowing green eyes was sighted roaming the hillside that night, wandering among the carnage of dead and dying men.

What Old Green Eyes might have been doing there depends on exactly what sort of entity it is. Some think it a demon, while others believe it to be the disembodied spirit of a dead soldier. Perhaps the most unusual theory is that the creature is a ghost tiger—the psychic embodiment of Union General Emerson Opdycke's brigade, which earned the title "Opdycke's Tigers" for its ferocity in battle. The eyewitness accounts, however, lead one to a different conclusion.

Visitors and rangers at the military park have described Old Green Eyes as a large, hairy creature. Its eyes are an unearthly greenish-orange color, and its teeth seem larger and sharper than human teeth—more like fangs. It has even been described as wearing simple clothing, perhaps even a long, flowing cloak.

Indian legends tell of similar two-legged creatures roaming the area long before the arrival of the white man. These are described as large, powerful, and human-like but definitely not one of our kind.

Scholars, while taking note of such tales, often scoff at them and dismiss them as morbid nature fantasies. Yet the Indians inhabited this land far longer than the white man and were familiar with every plant and animal in the forest—and the other things that roam there. One should not dismiss such stories lightly.

If Old Green Eyes is one of these hulking humanoids, then his presence on Snodgrass Hill might have a simple, if ghoulish, explanation: He was hungry. What for men of the North and South was a tragic loss of life was, for Old Green Eyes, a royal feast.

Thousands of dead from the battle were collected and given decent burials elsewhere, yet thousands more remained missing and unaccounted for. Where did they all go? Perhaps Old Green Eyes and his relatives know.

To this day, reports of this creature—whatever it is—continue at the Chickamauga battlefield. In the 1970s, visitors driving through the military park sighted Old Green Eyes on a number of occasions. Some of the drivers, panicking at the sight of the beast, wrecked their autos. The odd thing is that the sightings and subsequent accidents always occurred at the same spot.

Park rangers have also spotted the creature. One former park employee, Ranger Tinney, swore he saw it at close range one dark and foggy night while making his rounds. The beast crossed the path less than seven yards ahead of the ranger, remained for a moment, and then was gone again. The green-eyed beast had merged into the mist, but Ranger Tinney had gotten a clear glimpse of him.

Other things not easily explained also happen in the park. There are persistent reports of a disembodied head floating over the field near Snodgrass Hill, said to be all that is left of a Rebel soldier blown to pieces by Union artillery. On foggy nights, it drifts over the hillside, moaning and groaning, looking for the rest of its body.

Specters abound elsewhere on the battlefield, too. Hunting in the park is forbidden, yet people have often heard the sound of distant gunfire resounding over the fields. Are they echoes from far away, or perhaps echoes from a faraway time? At different places in the park, some have claimed to hear the groaning of wounded men. At times, the screams and groans seem almost like a ghostly chorus of pain.

Finally, there is the Lady in White, a female phantom thought to be the sweetheart of a soldier lost in the fury of battle. In life she roamed the battlefield in search of her lost love, and now in death she continues her mournful quest.

They say that, unlike money, you can take glory with you; but valor has its price. For many of those who fought and died at Chickamauga, their spirits have yet to free themselves from the memories of their earthbound agonies. They continue to experience those three hellish days, doomed to fight on in eternal battle.

35

THE VAMPIRE OF
BRADLEY COUNTY

A FEW MILES EAST OF THE TOWN OF
Charleston, in Bradley County, Tennessee, the Upper
River Road winds in and out among the hills overlooking
the Hiwassee River.

In the second decade of the twentieth century, just
before the Great War, the county was engaged in improv-
ing the roads in the area. One day, while widening the
Upper River Road, a work crew made an unusual discovery.

The men were busily removing rock and dust with
their picks and shovels when they uncovered the body of
an adult female, which had become petrified. That
would have been strange enough in itself, but there was
a wooden stake—also petrified—driven straight through
her heart.

The body had been in the ground for some time, although no one could tell just how long. Nor could anyone explain how it had become petrified. Then, too, the
matter of the stake in her heart was mystifying. Obviously, someone had cause to believe that the woman was
a vampire and had taken action to correct the situation.

Such an occurrence surely would have drawn the attention of neighbors in the small community. Yet an investigation conducted locally turned up no reports or
even a rumor of such an incident of vampirism.

The portion of the Upper River Road where the discovery was made lay on land owned by the Camp family.
William and John Camp had both been officers in the
Confederate army and had served honorably and well in
the Civil War. Their grandchildren had heard no tales of
vampirism or anything like it in the area, and if the Camp
brothers knew anything about the petrified vampire on
their property, they took the secret to their graves with
them.

The mountains of East Tennessee and the Tennessee
Valley are chock-full of tales of ghosts and goblins,
witches and boogers, but there is nary a hint of any stories concerning vampires. In all the lore of Appalachia,
the vampire is notably absent. This makes the discovery
near the town of Charleston all the more strange.

To this day, no one has solved the mystery of the
Vampire of Bradley County.

MEMPHIS IN MAYHEM:
UNCANNY ENCOUNTERS ALONG
THE BIG MUDDY AND
IN WEST TENNESSEE

36

THE GHOST OF GRACELAND

ONCE UPON A TIME, A GREAT KING DWELT in his palace in the opulent city of ancient Memphis, by the banks of the broad brown Nile. When he died, there was wailing and a gnashing of teeth, and there were signs and wonders upon his passing. In modern Memphis, by the banks of the broad brown Mississippi, another great "King" died, and once more there was wailing and a gnashing of teeth—and in the home of this King there also were signs and wonders.

It is said that when a great man dies, the very heaven and earth mark his passing, reflecting the turmoil and grief over his death. August 16, 1977, is a date that is seared in the memory of many people as the Day Elvis Died. To some, it is a doubly distressing date, for it marks not only the day of Elvis Presley's passing but also the day they had their own supernatural encounter with the King of Rock 'n' Roll.

There is no denying that Elvis possessed an incredible charisma—it was part and parcel of his musical genius. And if even a fraction of the reports about encounters with him since 1977 are true, his personal magnetism and charisma have grown even stronger from beyond the grave.

Encounters with the spirit of Elvis run the gamut from the supernatural to the truly bizarre. But whatever one may think of the nature of these encounters, there is little doubt that the majority of those who have reported their experiences with the ghost of Elvis are absolutely sincere.

Encounters with the spirit of Elvis began almost from the moment he passed over. Take the case of Lynn Harper, for example. On the morning of August 16, 1977, she was lying in bed around 8 A.M., letting her mind wander before getting up for the day. As she lay there, idly daydreaming, a series of vivid images suddenly flooded her mind. For no particular reason, she started to reflect on Elvis Presley and his life, and in a flash, those random thoughts turned into a whole series of visions. She saw a sick and pale Elvis, then the image him in his coffin. Next she saw the King, in brilliant Technicolor, reunited with his mother, which Lynn interpreted as a vision of heaven.

Later that day, Lynn heard the news about Elvis's death. It was only then that she realized the full significance of the vision she had experienced.

That same day, around noon, a midwestern businessman had left his office for lunch and a breath of fresh air. As he was standing out on the street, talking with a friend, the notion that Elvis had died suddenly popped into his head. He had not listened to the radio at all, nor had he read the paper that day—it was simply a case of pure intuition.

That afternoon, an elderly farmer—we'll call him "Claude"—was tending his livestock on his farm in the countryside east of Memphis. Claude had known Elvis when he was a young lad, before he made it big. Over the years, Elvis had kept in touch and paid occasional visits to his old friend, and once even helped Claude out when money got tight.

Claude was seeing to an injured calf out in the field when he saw Elvis coming up the hill toward him. The farmer thought he saw a blue fog around Elvis at first, but he didn't think much of it for it had been such a long time since he had seen his friend.

When Elvis got closer, Claude asked him what he was doing there. Elvis told him that he'd come to say good-bye. At that point, the farmer was going to say something to the King when he was distracted by the sound of his wife's voice coming from the farmhouse down the hill. Claude turned away to look at her for an instant, and when he turned back around, Elvis had vanished without a trace.

When the old farmer got back to the house to see why his wife had called him, he found her in tears. The radio had just announced that their old friend, Elvis Presley, was dead!

That night, two women in Kentucky, both loyal Elvis fans, returned to one's apartment to mourn their loss and listen to old Elvis records. Both had been in a state of shock since hearing of the King's death but had been unable to do much about it until they got off work. Entering the apartment, they found that the woman's prized collection of Elvis records—a complete collection that included every song he had ever recorded-had dissolved into a molten mass of vinyl. Nothing else in the apartment was damaged, just the Elvis records. And upon further inspection, the women realized that the discs had melted while still in their cardboard sleeves inside the record cabinet!

In the South, and around the country, people—some fans and some not—reported strange and mystifying encounters the day Elvis Presley died. Dr. Ray Moody, a respected clinical psychologist, has documented these and similar encounters. But Elvis' death was only the beginning, for ever since that fateful August day, people from all walks of life have had uncanny encounters with the Undead Elvis.

Oddly, despite the tabloid press's continuing fascination with Elvis, the supermarket weeklies have rarely reported on ghostly encounters with the King. Instead, the tabloids have generally focused on sightings by persons claiming to have seen Presley still "alive." Gail Brewer-Giorgio, one of the leading Elvisologists in the world, has documented many of these sightings in a series of books.

While Brewer-Giorgio makes a strong case for the "live" Elvis sightings, enough evidence has accumulated to prove conclusively that the legendary entertainer did indeed die in 1977. That being the case, a number of the eyewitness reports she has collected should more properly be considered ghostly encounters. Both Moody and Brewer-Giorgio have documented cases of Elvis haunting the nation's highways, especially in parts of the country that were his old haunts during his life—West Tennessee, northern Mississippi, Louisiana, and Arkansas.

While one might be tempted to dismiss these reports as simply the work of Elvis impersonators, more difficult to dismiss is the phantom phone call that Dee Presley, a relative, received in 1978. One night, Dee picked up the phone and talked with a stranger who did not identify himself but whose voice resembled Elvis's. The mysterious caller also knew things about the King and his family that only Elvis could have known. Other celebrities who were familiar with Elvis have also received mysterious phone calls of a similar nature.

Of course, the most credible accounts of Elvis Presley's apparition emanate from his famed mansion in Memphis, Graceland. Sightings at Graceland began soon after the King's death. Not long after the house and grounds were opened to the public, a visitor named Lorraine Hartz encountered the fully materialized image of the King on the grounds of the estate.

Other visitors since then have also reported seeing his apparition. One tourist claimed to have seen the King's ghostly visage in the bath house, near poolside, and another reported seeing Presley riding about the grounds on horseback. Still other visitors have encountered the King in the meditation garden near his grave.

Then there is a whole series of reports from individuals who claim to have seen Elvis's image looking out at them from a window at Graceland. In February 1985, a tourist from the British Isles snapped a photograph outside Graceland that revealed a face peering out of a downstairs window—and that face looks for all the world like Elvis Presley.

Likewise, in May 1987, a couple from Missouri toured Graceland. Toward the end of the tour, the husband, Jacob, went back in front of the mansion to take a few parting shots. He was about to snap a picture when he saw Elvis peering out a corner window on the second floor. Needless to say, the tourist was "all shook up"!

There are also reports concerning the Phantom Limousine. These sightings, which most often occur at about 2:30 A.M., involve a large black limo that appears at the gates of Graceland. Visitors close to the entrance have sworn they have seen Elvis inside the Phantom Limousine as it passed by them.

Beyond the sightings, many more people have reported coming away from their visit to Graceland with a very strong feeling that Elvis's "presence" dominates the entire mansion and grounds. Several have said they had the feeling that they might at any moment walk around a corner and come face to face with Elvis. Even Presley's half-brother, Billy Stanley, visiting the mansion after several years' absence, said he felt the continuing presence of the King, adding, "To this day, his spirit is still at Graceland."

It has been over twenty years since the King died, yet Elvis is bigger now than ever. Graceland has become a permanent shrine to a figure who now approaches mythic status. They say that Elvis has left the building—but has he?

37

A DARK, DARK DAY
IN MEMPHIS

WHEN IS A CLOUD NOT A CLOUD, AND A storm not a storm? Perhaps no one can answer that riddle, but if you had been living in Memphis in December 1904, you just might have been able to understand the question.

The second day of December dawned clear and cold in the Bluff City. Working people, black and white, went about their daily business, while mothers fed their children and then saw that they got off to school on time. The docks bustled with the usual Friday morning activities as laborers loaded and unloaded whitewashed sternwheelers and other vessels. All in all, it was a typical morning in the busy river port of Memphis.

About nine o'clock, however, all that changed when, suddenly, without warning, the sun was blotted from the sky.

In the space of a minute or so, the city went from bright, sunlit autumn morn to utter and complete darkness. All work came to a crashing halt. For several long minutes, workers scrambled in the dark to find their gas lamps or incandescent lights, and those with neither had to make do with old-fashioned oil lamps, if they could.

It was immediately apparent that the blanket of darkness covering the city was no ordinary cloud. It was not just some somber gray overcast but an "inky darkness" that descended over the region like a shroud. One report compared the darkness to the blackness of midnight.

Around Court House Square, the squirrels scurried to their treetop homes, while birds throughout the city sought their usual nightly roosts.

At the Electric Light Company, the meters soon began to register dramatic power drains as homes and offices began to flip on their incandescent lamps. Workers at the power plant were obliged to throw open the clutches on several of the big dynamos to keep up with the sudden demand.

Elsewhere in Memphis, reactions were varied to the "strange visitation of darkness." Even men whom the papers described as being "of cool judgment and ordinarily good sense" were "sorely puzzled," to say the least. Others, however, had much stronger reactions.

Few of the city's schools had any lighting other than sunlight and were thus instantly plunged into the dark abyss. Many children were badly frightened, despite teachers' attempts to calm them.

In homes throughout the city, many women and small children, alone and without any outside contact, became panicky in the intense dark. Several mothers stifled their own fears in order to calm their children, while other women gave in to their fears and became hysterical.

Physicians were kept busy throughout the strange event and afterward, attending to those persons, young and old, who fell victim to panic attacks as a result of the day that turned to night. Some, turning to the Bible, saw in this uncanny event the biblical prophecies fulfilled. Many throughout the city began to believe the end of the world was at hand. Down on the levee, the stevedores and other laborers were also disoriented and alarmed by the death of the sun.

The conservative *Commercial Appeal* made much of the fact that one dockworker, an elderly Negro, was terrified out of his wits by the darkness. According to the newspaper, the man clung for dear life, hugging a nearby telegraph pole, convinced the end was nigh. Even after the darkness had finally lifted and real storm clouds were rapidly coming up, the ancient Negro was still too scared to move, the paper said. Finally, a young black longshoreman dashed out of his shelter and dragged the elderly man to safety.

The terror and panic was by no means limited to the black population. At least as many and perhaps more whites became terrified and confused. Nor were their fears unfounded.

After shrouding the city in total darkness for a solid half-hour, the blackness over Memphis lifted as quickly as it had descended. No one quite knew what had happened, but everyone was relieved when the ordeal finally passed. But the question remains: What exactly was it they had experienced?

The authorities and newspapers, hastening to calm a jittery public, dismissed the event as just a storm cloud— if they mentioned it at all. But detailed contemporary accounts make it clear that whatever descended on the city was unlike any storm cloud ever seen over Memphis before or since.

The sudden and unexpected onset of darkness and the utter blackening of the heavens do not square with any sort of natural weather system. Bad weather can cause much fear and anxiety, but even the worst storm would not cause so many people to think that the end of the world was at hand.

If it was not a cloud, then what was it? Charles Fort, who researched this and similar unexplained phenomena, was also dubious as to the conventional "cloud" explanation. Writing in the early decades of this century, he leaned toward the theory that the Dark Day in Memphis—and related events elsewhere in time and place— were due to "unscheduled" eclipses.

As neither the moon, the sun, nor the other planets have ever been known to take a vacation, Fort theorized that some unobserved celestial object, or as he put it, "unknown dark bodies," may have passed near enough to earth to totally blot out the sun's rays over a large area on earth. There is much to recommend Fort's theory—it certainly makes more sense than what government publications like the *Monthly Weather Report* had to say on the subject.

There is, however, one major flaw in Fort's theory that the darkness was due to a passing asteroid or comet. For one thing, even a total solar eclipse rarely lasts more than three minutes, and while that darkness is indeed almost like evening, it is not an "inky darkness," such as that which descended on Memphis.

Even assuming that a comet or large asteroid came close enough to create that effect, it would have to have been in a very near-earth orbit, hovering directly over the vicinity of Memphis without moving. Any object of that size coming that close to the earth would surely have caused major tidal disturbances, and gravity would inevitably draw it down to the earth's surface—as many scientists believe happened when the dinosaurs were wiped out—in which case, we would not be alive to contemplate this strange occurrence.

Because all celestial objects are constantly in motion, it would have been impossible for any naturally occurring celestial body to hover over a given spot on earth. Only an object that is both self-propelled and capable of resisting the force of gravity could do that.

The implications of all this are enormous—and so was the size of the spaceship that hovered over Memphis on a December day in 1904.

38

LITTLE GIRL LOST

SHOULD YOU EVER GO TO MEMPHIS, BE sure to visit the Orpheum Theater. Built in 1928, the stately structure reflects all the charm of that era—ornate gilded decoration, plush seats, and a massive chandelier which seems to float high above the audience in midair. But if you go to a show there, whatever you do, don't sit in seat C-5, because that seat is reserved for Mary.

Many people in Memphis are familiar with Mary; she is the theater's unofficial "mascot," for one thing. Mary looks to be about twelve years old. She wears a white school uniform, has brown pigtails and long black stockings, and possesses a mischievous sense of humor. In short, Mary is a typical twelve-year-old, save for one thing—she died in 1921.

Nobody is quite sure how or why Mary began haunting the Orpheum, but for as long as anyone can remember, she has been there. Mary attends almost every show staged in the theater, and she often stays afterward to mix with the cast and tease the work crews. For many years, management tried to keep Mary's presence in the theater a secret. It was felt that it would be bad for business if word got out that the theater was haunted.

In the 1960s, Harlan Judkin was involved in a project to restore the theater's ornate pipe organ. He had never heard any ghost stories about the place and was a skeptic by nature. Harlan and his associates had to wait until the late movie was over on Saturday nights to work on the massive instrument.

One Saturday after the show, Harlan and two of his co-workers were struggling to overcome what seemed to be an insoluble problem in the upper right-hand organ chamber housing the pipes. Try as they might, there seemed no way to fix it. Fatigued and at the end of their wits, the three men took a break and went across the street to have a cup of coffee. When they returned, to their amazement, they found the organ was already repaired.

The three were mystified—there was no way the organ could have repaired itself. As they were gathering up their tools and discussing the strange happening, all three were suddenly overcome by an icy feeling. They looked at each other—all had felt it at the same time—and one exclaimed, "There's somebody else up here." But no other living being was anywhere in the theater.

Harlan had other unusual experiences while working on the organ, but it was only after the project was completed that he heard about the theater being haunted. He soon met others who had experienced similar strange events in the theater. His encounters were not isolated incidents, after all.

In 1970, Vincent Astor became director of operations for the theater. The local community had begun to realize what a gem the old building was and made efforts to restore it. Vincent's attitude toward Mary was considerably different from that of his predecessor. Instead of suppressing talk of the Orpheum's ghost, Vincent acknowledged Mary's existence and embraced her as part of the theater's long heritage.

Most of the encounters involving Mary have taken the form of minor incidents—or coincidences. In 1976, for example, Ballet South was holding rehearsals in the old theater. One evening, after rehearsals were over, a young ballerina named Anna went to call her father for a ride home. The pay phone was located in the lower lobby, which was in complete darkness except for a dim light within the phone booth itself.

The ballerina picked her way through the gloom,

very jittery about being down there in the dark alone. As she made her call, Anna thought to herself how much more secure she would feel if the lights were on. When she emerged from the booth, all the lights came on, as if someone or something had turned them on for her. Was it Mary? The young ballerinas of Ballet South are convinced that it was.

At times, the Orpheum's pipe organ begins playing all by itself. No song, really, more like random notes—much as a child untutored in music would play them. This has been known to occur even when the organ is switched off.

A volunteer named Brad who has helped with the electrical repairs around the theater has reported the sound of a "female soprano voice" singing in the building late at night. A maintenance worker also has seen a young girl dart down the theater aisles late at night. On other occasions, workers have caught fleeting glimpses of a girl in darkened hallways or wandering the upper aisles of the balcony.

Performers on stage at the Orpheum have also spotted Mary, dressed in a little white uniform and sitting in seat C-5. In 1977, when the New York road company of *Fiddler on the Roof* played the theater, members of the cast immediately became aware of her presence. The actors later went so far as to hold a séance in the upper balcony after opening night.

Perhaps the most dramatic encounter with Mary occurred in April 1979 when Vincent Astor was regaling a small group of visitors late one night. As Vincent was playing on the organ, the theater turned ice cold. From experience, Astor knew that Mary was fond of the song "Never, Never Land," and each time he began playing it, the theater became as cold as a tomb. Some of the group thought they saw a faint light come from the lobby and then jump down behind some seats in the back.

One member of the group, Theresa, felt compelled to investigate. She had an overwhelming sense that something was out there, and when she and two others looked toward the lobby, they saw the figure of a little girl with brown hair dancing to the sound of the music.

Theresa stepped closer, half afraid the girl would disappear and half afraid she wouldn't. Theresa seemed uncontrollably drawn to the apparition. Finally, she halted midway across the lobby, too filled with dread to approach any closer.

Two other members of the group did try to catch up with the dancing girl, but she disappeared just as they got to the spot. Just then, there was a furious clatter and rattle in the nearby broom closet. Neither dared open it, and when they rejoined the rest of the group, the rattling stopped.

But when the rattling ceased, the little girl returned. Altogether, the incident lasted over three-quarters of an hour, far longer than any other known appearance by Mary. Long after the figure of the girl had disappeared, the intense icy cold and the feeling of being watched persisted.

At other times, a local glossy magazine has paid a visit to the theater for Halloween, and a parapsychology class from the University of Memphis has tried to communicate with Mary. From what she allegedly told the students, Mary died in a "falling accident" in 1921 somewhere in the downtown area. Her spirit just wandered into the Orpheum and never left.

The crowds, bright lights, happy music, and make-believe environment of the theater are attractive to the lost and lonely spirit of a young girl who died unexpectedly. Vincent Astor thinks that, because she died so suddenly, Mary does not know what to do with herself. He believes that ghosts like Mary decide they "don't believe" what happened to them and so have become "stuck" on the earthly plane.

Mary continues to dwell in the "Never, Never Land" of the Orpheum Theater, which has now become her home. To Mary, it is those of us who pass through her world for a few short hours that are the real phantoms—not she.

39

THE CURSE OF THE ROSE BEDROOM

IN DOWNTOWN MEMPHIS, SEVERAL blocks from the Orpheum Theater but close in spirit, is the district known as the Victorian Village. It consists of a row of perfectly preserved Victorian-era townhomes and mansions on Adams Avenue and surrounding streets. Preserved as house museums, a number of these homes are open to the public—and a number of them are haunted.

Of particular note is the Fontaine House at 680 Adams Avenue. Here, the sad spirit of a resident has returned to haunt her home of many years and many tears. For here is where Mollie Woodruff suffered through the Curse of the Rose Bedroom.

Constructed in 1871 by Amos Woodruff, the mansion reflects the opulent lifestyle of the Memphis merchant class of that time. Built in French Victorian style, with an ornate mansard roof, the three-story house has eighteen-foot ceilings on the main floor and an abundance of hand-carved woodwork and elaborate crystal chandeliers. In its heyday, the cream of Memphis society graced the home's parlors and ballroom.

Amos Woodruff had four children, and of these, Mollie was the apple of his eye. Nothing was too good or too expensive for Amos's firstborn. But sometimes, not even wealth, power, or influence is enough to assure one's happiness.

On the face of it, Mollie should have been the happiest of girls. As a child, she enjoyed an almost a fairytale life. She lived in a large gingerbread "cottage" with servants to wait on her and had every toy a little girl could hope for. Her doting father saw to her every want and desire.

On December 13, 1871, not long after the Woodruffs moved into the large new mansion, Mollie married Egbert Wooldridge. They were a happy couple, by all accounts, and began their life together in a suite of rooms on the second floor of Amos's spacious home. In February 1875, their union was blessed by the birth of a child, delivered in a second-floor bedroom known as the Rose Bedroom.

Mollie and Egbert's bliss proved short-lived, however. The infant soon contracted yellow fever and died—in the Rose Bedroom.

Several months later, Mollie's husband went on a fishing trip down the Mississippi. While on the trip, he was involved in a boating accident and nearly drowned. Suffering from exposure, Wooldridge contracted pneumonia, and when he returned home to Mollie, he took to his bed, fell into a coma and died—in the Rose Bedroom.

It was some years before Mollie recovered from this double loss. But she was still young and pretty, and the most eligible bachelors eagerly sought her hand. Finally, Mollie married James Henning, and again Mollie and her husband moved into the house on Adams Avenue after the honeymoon.

Once more, the union was blessed with a child, but the firstborn of this marriage also contracted yellow fever and died—in the Rose Bedroom.

In 1883, the Woodruffs moved out of the house at 680 Adams, selling it to Noland Fontaine. Some say that a reversal of Old Amos's fortunes were to blame, but the truth was that his daughter Mollie had experienced too much pain and loss there, and the house was filled with those sorrowful memories.

Mollie may have moved, but no change of scene could erase her memories of the house and the Rose Bedroom. Some say that when Mollie Woodruff Henning died in 1917, she moved back into the house at 680 Adams Avenue.

Today, the Woodruff-Fontaine House is managed by the Memphis Museum System and serves as the centerpiece of the organization's Victorian Village. Visitors can step back in time and see what life was like in a middle-class home in the late nineteenth century. There is no additional charge for the ghosts.

Strange stories have been circulating about the house for many years, according to Virginia Ingle, curator of the museum. A ghostly presence is most often felt in the second-floor bedroom where the two infants and Mollie's first husband all passed away. It is commonly believed that the presence is Mollie, still grieving over her loss and unable to depart.

There are times when the room becomes icy cold for no apparent reason. Then the cold will suddenly go away, and the room will feel nice and warm again. At other times, the Rose Bedroom will become saturated with a musty smell, but the staff can never find a reason for it.

A focal point for some of the strange happenings in the Rose Bedroom seems to be the bed that once belonged to Mollie Woodruff Henning. The bed always seems to be rumpled, as if someone had been sitting or lying on it. Virginia Ingle has personally straightened the bedsheets many times, only to find them rumpled again a few minutes later. Sometimes, the sheets seem to form the silhouette of a human body—much like someone were asleep on top of the bed.

The room has also been the source of strange noises on occasion. One morning, around ten o'clock, two of the museum interpreters, Scarlett and Ted, were downstairs when they heard what sounded like a woman's muffled crying. At first they did not pay much heed to it, but the crying went on for some twenty minutes, so the two staffers finally went up the stairs to investigate.

When the two reached the first landing, however, the sobbing stopped. As they walked around the bedroom, everything looked normal, but when they went back downstairs, the crying started again. Ted and Scarlett later found that the psychic event had occurred one day before the anniversary of Wooldridge's death in the Rose Bedroom. Was Mollie reliving the moment of her husband's death?

On other occasions, a voice can be heard in the room sighing, "my dear, my dear."

On three separate occasions, psychics have visited the house, and each has seen a woman in the Rose Bedroom. Later, each was able to pick out a photo of Mollie from a "lineup."

A tourist visiting the museum once wandered into the Rose Bedroom. Although visitors generally are not told about the haunting in the building, this person needed no such warning. As soon as she walked into the bedroom, she began to have a hard time breathing. Instinctively, she turned to the guide and asked, "Who died in this room?"

On another occasion, a child around the age of seven visiting the house with a school group was staring intently at the room as the tour guide gave her lecture. As the children were about to leave, the student turned and pointed to the rocking chair in the bedroom and asked, "Hey, what happened to the lady who was sitting there?" Ingle and the teacher were the only adults present, and both had been in the hallway and not the room during the episode.

Specters have been reported roaming other parts of the house as well, but it is in the Rose Bedroom that the majority of the spectral encounters have occurred.

Upstairs and downstairs, the memories of yesterday linger at Fontaine House. So tread lightly if you go there, lest you disturb Mollie in her mournful reveries—or raise the ire of her upstairs relatives. For in the house on Adams Avenue, the uncommon and the unearthly are commonplace.

40

THE DAY IT RAINED SNAKES

EIGHTEEN SEVENTY-SIX WAS A BAD YEAR for weather in Kentucky—the shower of blood and gore showed that—but January 1877 in Memphis, Tennessee, proved to be equally bizarre.

It was a cold winter on the Mississippi; the river was frozen solid up beyond Fort Pillow, and ice floes hindered traffic downstream. Cold weather was to be expected in January, of course, even in Memphis. What was not expected, however, was for it to rain snakes.

A change in the weather finally occurred on Monday, January 15, when temperatures rose and rain fell on the southern sections of Memphis. It was a hard, driving rain, the water descending in torrents. But in one particular area of the city's south side, the precipitation came down a bit harder than elsewhere, for it seems that, along with the rain, came a downpour of wriggling, writhing snakes.

The serpentine shower was quite heavy, for there were snakes by the thousands on the ground soon after. The snakes were all dark brown—almost black—in color, and were quite large for airborne serpents. They averaged between a foot and foot and a half in length—not huge, but then such creatures rarely fly through the air.

So many snakes rained down in the space of a few blocks that there were still large numbers of the reptiles on the ground for the next several days. The event attracted some attention at the time; the story was picked up by *The New York Times*, and some scholarly journals took note as well.

No rational explanation was possible, of course, but that did not stop the pundits from trying to invent one. *Scientific American* theorized that "they were probably carried aloft by a hurricane," but the publication confessed that where snakes existed in such numbers was a mystery.

Besides, January is not hurricane season, nor do hurricanes reach as far inland as Memphis. More curiously, snakes are cold-blooded animals and would be underground, lying dormant, during the winter months. How, then, could even a whirlwind have sucked them up—and done so by the thousands—and deposited them on the streets of Memphis?

In the end, all rational explanations seem to fail, and all attempts to square the facts with the laws of science end in absurdity. A century ago, Ambrose Bierce, writing about another strange mystery, posed the rhetorical question that still faces us: "Can Such Things Be?"

Yes, indeed they can!

CHRIS COLEMAN received his undergraduate degree in history at St. Anselm College in Manchester, New Hampshire, and pursued graduate work in archaeology at the University of Chicago. He has produced award-winning documentaries and commercials, and served as executive director of a cultural agency in Sumner County, Tennessee, where he supervised community and folk arts projects. More recently, Coleman has been active in the publishing industry. He and his wife, Veronica, reside in Hendersonville, Tennessee, with their four children, four cats, one dog, and no ghosts.